THE MAN
GOD USES

THE MAN GOD USES

HENRY AND TOM BLACKABY

BROADMAN
&HOLMAN
PUBLISHERS

Nashville, Tennessee

0–8054–2145–9

Published by Broadman & Holman Publishers, Nashville, Tennessee
Editorial Team: Leonard G. Goss, John Landers, Sandra Bryer
Page Design and Typesetting: TF Designs, Mt. Juliet, Tennessee

Dewey Decimal Classification: 248
Subject Heading: MEN—–RELIGIOUS LIFE

Unless otherwise noted, Scripture quotations are from the Holy Bible,
New International Version, copyright 1973, 1978, 1984.
Passages marked NKJV are from the New King James Version,
copyright 1979, 1980, 1982, Thomas Nelson, Inc., Publishers.

Library of Congress Cataloging-in-Publication Data

Blackaby, Henry T., 1935–
    The man God uses / Henry and Tom Blackaby.
          p.   cm.
    ISBN 0–8054–2145–9
    1. Christian men--Religious life.   I. Blackaby, Tom, 1962–
    II. Title.
    BV4528.2.B57 1999
    248.8'42--dc21

                            99-37776
                              CIP

4 5 6 7 8 9 10 05 04 03 02 01 00

CONTENTS

AUTHORS

Henry Blackaby is special assistant to the presidents of the following agencies of the Southern Baptist Convention: LifeWay Christian Resources, International Mission Board, and North American Mission Board. Henry was a pastor in the Los Angeles area before accepting a call to Faith Baptist Church in Saskatoon, Saskatchewan. Henry wrote *What the Spirit Is Saying to the Churches,* the story of God's activity among his people at Faith Baptist Church, and *Experiencing God,* a study that encourages believers to find out where God is working and join him. Henry has written for numerous publications and has led conferences in the United States, Canada, and around the world. Henry and his wife Marilynn have five children: Richard, Thomas, Melvin, Norman, and Carrie. All five children have responded to God's call to church-related ministry or missions.

Although *Tom Blackaby* was born in California, he spent his formative years in Saskatoon, Sask., Canada. Tom currently serves as a pastor in British Columbia, Canada. He has served churches in combination positions as minister of youth, music, and education in three countries, including two years in Stavanger, Norway. He is married to Kim and has two children, Erin and Matthew. Tom has acted as music editor for *Anchor in the Storm* by Mike McElroy as well as on the Advisory Board for *Songs for Praise and Worship,* Word Music, Inc. Tom currently volunteers as Discipleship/Family Ministries Consultant for the

Canadian Convention of Southern Baptists. Tom and his family make their home in Vancouver, B.C., Canada.

PREFACE

Men's hearts are feeling a tremendous surge of God's activity today. It is as if God has announced: "The world has had my people long enough! I am calling them back to me. I will mold them and shape them for my purposes in my world!" Men are responding to this call, and God is transforming men across our nation.

Many men understand this quickening of their souls and know precisely what God is asking of them. They are responding with a resounding, "Yes, Lord!" Others know God is speaking but are unclear as to how they should respond. Yet others recognize a deep stirring in their lives but do not recognize it is God.

This book is put together with much prayer and heart-searching, that strong, clear help and encouragement may come to those lives God is touching. There is no question in our minds that if thousands of men "return to God" and God in turn returns to them (Zech. 1:3), great revival will come through them and have worldwide impact.

Be assured of our sincere prayer and intercession as you study this material either personally or in an interactive, accountability group. May God receive the highest glory and honor to his name as we offer this book for his use to draw his people back to himself.

I want to acknowledge my deepest indebtedness to my son, Tom. This study is a combination of our life ministries and experiences with God's people. Tom encouraged me with his incredible ability to write and communicate, from his heart, the central truths of God's "good news" for men. I am grateful to Tom's wife, Kim, and to my wife, Marilynn, for their constant support. I am grateful to the many men over the years who have sought so earnestly to be God's men in their homes, in churches, and in the marketplace where God has placed them. To Sam House, a good friend and godly man, who patiently tailored our work, we will be forever grateful. Sam's heart is displayed throughout this book as he has clarified and infused his experiences and insight concerning God's word and his activity among men.

May your life be drawn closer to God and may it be forever changed for his glory and his use as you study the Scriptures and truths found in this book.

Henry T. Blackaby

INTRODUCTION

Welcome to *The Man God Uses*. As you turn these pages, we want you to do more than read a book. We want you to be involved, to work with the Scriptures, and to consider what it means to be a godly man. As you begin this book, consider the following.

1. Pay careful attention to the Scripture shared in these pages. Spend time meditating on and discussing with others what God is revealing to you through each Scripture.

2. Trust the Holy Spirit to be your teacher and guide. Release your mind and heart in ready obedience to all he will teach you.

3. Pray sincerely, basing your prayers on what the Holy Spirit has revealed to you through the Scriptures you read.

4. Keep a spiritual journal of God's activity in your life as well as your response to him. When God speaks, record it. Your memory will not always recall these special moments, but your journal will!

5. Live out your growing relationship and knowledge of God in your daily life. Share this freely with others. Expect God to honor your faithful obedience to him.

To gain even more from this book, read each chapter, then meet with a group of men who are also reading the book to process what you are learning.

Chapter 1

THE CHARACTER
OF THE MAN GOD USES

God chose the foolish things of the world to shame the wise;
God chose the weak things of the world to shame the strong.
He chose the lowly things of this world and the despised things.

—1 Corinthians 1:27–28

God is known for taking the ordinary and making it extraordinary. Throughout Scripture God used ordinary men to affect his kingdom in extraordinary ways.

One thing, however, set them apart. If we look carefully, we can see something they had in common. Each man God used had a responsive heart ready to hear God and a life that was available to obey God. Each also possessed the integrity to honor God.

Talent and ability are not prerequisites to being used by God. Accomplishments, awards, and recognition will not ensure kingdom usefulness; a "broken and contrite heart" does (Ps. 51:17). The Lord looks at the condition of a man's heart.

> "I the LORD search the heart
> and examine the mind."
>
> (Jer. 17:10)

Two things are involved in taking the ordinary and making it extraordinary: a man and Almighty God in a covenant relationship. We are the ordinary. The extraordinary comes from God's nature. Whatever God touches becomes special because the Creator has interacted with the creation.

Each party has a role to fulfill in a relationship. But, unlike a human contract which becomes void if one party defaults, God never fails. God is faithful regardless of our faithfulness. However, some conditions must be met before God will use us.

> AVAILABILITY—THE STATE OF BEING
> READY FOR USE.

Because God is everywhere, any situation has the potential for becoming extraordinary. His presence dramatically changes the circumstances. There is no limit to what will happen. From man's perspective this process is unexplainable. From a kingdom perspective it is the normal way God accomplishes his will through us.

> "'No eye has seen,
>   no ear has heard,
> no mind has conceived
>   what God has prepared for those who love him.'"
>
> (1 Cor. 2:9)

When I go to a doctor for a physical examination, he checks my blood pressure and heart rate, takes blood samples, and asks about any aches and pains. He checks for warning signs of heart disease, stroke, or any hidden ailments. Although physical checkups are common to men my age, spiritual checkups are less common.

If we fail to heed the warning signs, spiritual sickness will grow just like a physical disease. Our spiritual hearts will weaken and fail us. A weakening heart, whether physical or spiritual, puts us in crisis and makes us a possible candidate for surgery.

The Holy Spirit may point to symptoms that indicate a larger problem. God's Spirit may ask you to stop and deal with a particular issue in your character or behavior.

The Bible is full of spiritual checkups to help us stay on track and in good spiritual health. Psalm 15 is a great example of one of these spiritual checkups. Take a moment to read it now, slowly and thoughtfully.

This whole chapter deals with the heart. Consider it a heart "checkup" with the Great Physician, our Heavenly Father. If you sense the Holy Spirit dealing with you, stop immediately and listen carefully to him. Our prayer is that this book, with the leading of the Holy Spirit, will guide you into a healthy relationship with God.

A SPIRITUAL CHECKUP

David wrote,

> "Search me, O God, and know my heart;
>   test me and know my anxious thoughts.
> See if there is any offensive way in me,
>   and lead me in the way everlasting."

(Ps. 139:23–24)

Just as a doctor points out signs of your health and sickness during a physical checkup, the Holy Spirit will show you the condition of your heart. He can use Scripture and circumstances, among other things, to do it. And when he does, as when we receive our report from the doctor, along with signs of health, we may receive some bad news.

The good news is that God changes the hearts of men.

At age nineteen, miserable, tired of the gang culture he lived in, Fernando Hernandez gave his life to Christ. Since then, he has shared Christ through a gang-prevention ministry to youth.

"I tell them that it is easy to do the wrong thing," said Hernandez. "Anyone can pick up a rock and chuck it through a window. But only a man could go to the lady, and say, 'I broke your window,' and offer to pay for it and make it right." Fifteen years earlier, Fernando was a gang member. Today, Jesus lives through him, and his life is a testimony to the power of God to change lives.[1]

God is interested most of all in the condition of your heart. In Acts 13:22, God testifies that in David he found a man after his own heart, one whom he could count on to "do everything I want him to do." Would God find you to be such a man?

The development of a strong Christian character is the development of a man after God's own heart. Your character is who you are when no one is looking and what you are willing to stand for when someone is looking. Character is who you are striving to be and what you can be trusted with.

Integrity of character occurs when there is consistency between actions and inner convictions over time. Strong Christian character results from both human effort and divine intervention. It is the work of God as you relate to him in love.

Strong Christian character is the result of your heart's desires to obey God.

A PARADOX

First Corinthians 15:10 contains a great paradox. "By the grace of God I am what I am, and his grace to me was not without effect. No, I worked harder than all of them—yet not I, but the grace of God that was with me." Our character is developed fully by the power and grace of God which works within us. Yet, it is also a conscious decision we make to bring our mind, heart, and actions into line with God's will.

For instance, Al noticed a fellow employee taking home some items belonging to the company. When confronted, the fellow said that everyone did it; it was no big deal. Al replied that everyone did not do it. It was out of integrity that he did not do it. Noticing that the company items were fairly insignificant, Al asked, "Is your integrity only worth $2.50?" The employee said he had never thought of it that way and put the items back. Our character is a priceless possession that ought to be protected at all costs. It should never be for sale.

Hebrews 4:13 says, "Nothing in all creation is hidden from God's sight. Everything is uncovered and laid bare before the eyes of him to whom we must give account." God knows you inside and out. He knows your secret thoughts and feelings, your dreams and aspirations. God knows where your loyalties are and where your weaknesses cause you to stumble. He watches you interact with his people and react to circumstances. God looks to see if you are trustworthy and faithful. He can do much through you if your character is right.

If you are a man of little integrity or questionable character, do not expect God to reveal much of himself to you or to use you significantly for his kingdom. If you are a man of great character and integrity, you no doubt already have experienced God's activity in your life and serve him.

God is a mighty God who hears and saves us. But our sins separate us from God, and as a result, our relationship with him is not what it should be. All sins equally separate us from God—sins of doing wrong and sins of not doing right. Inaction and words can be as destructive as action and physical violence.

Consider the sins described in Isaiah 59:4:

> "No one calls for justice;
>   no one pleads his case with integrity.
> They rely on empty arguments and speak lies;
>   they conceive trouble and give birth to evil."

When truth becomes victim to preserving our own safety and comfort, or when rationales take the place of facts, we will find ourselves involved in sin.

QUALITIES OF GOOD CHARACTER

There are many different qualities of character. I want to introduce you to eight qualities of good character found in the man God uses.

HOLINESS

The prophet Isaiah saw God seated on a throne, high and exalted with angels flying about, calling to one another

> "'Holy, holy, holy is the LORD Almighty;
> the whole earth is full of his glory.'"
>
> (Isa. 6:3)

Immediately Isaiah cried out in despair because he recognized his sinfulness in the presence of a holy God. In the presence of God's holiness comes an awareness of our lack of holiness.

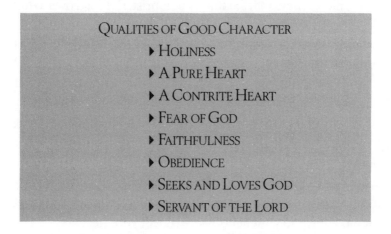

QUALITIES OF GOOD CHARACTER
- ▶ HOLINESS
- ▶ A PURE HEART
- ▶ A CONTRITE HEART
- ▶ FEAR OF GOD
- ▶ FAITHFULNESS
- ▶ OBEDIENCE
- ▶ SEEKS AND LOVES GOD
- ▶ SERVANT OF THE LORD

Holiness means "to be set apart and separate." We are to be separate from all that stains our world and dirties our lives—free of all sinful thoughts, destructive emotions, unclean images, impure motives, and questionable activities.

We cannot make ourselves holy. We can become holy only through the power of Christ and the working of the Holy Spirit in our lives. Through a pure and clean life, we reveal to our world the reality of holy God in our lives.

Isaiah 35:8 states that God is building a highway of holiness that the wicked cannot travel.

> "And a highway will be there
> > it will be called the Way of Holiness.
> The unclean will not journey on it;
> > it will be for those who walk in that Way;
> > wicked fools will not go about on it."

God desires that your life and mine be that highway, the road over which others may be drawn to Christ, the road over which God may bring revival to our land. All the prayers, sacrifices, and pleadings with God will not bring revival until we take seriously our holiness.

An impure heart and mind that fail to acknowledge sin are barriers to effectively praying and seeking the Lord. If we choose to fill our minds with pornography, violence, immorality, hatred, promiscuity, and self-centeredness and call it entertainment, God will not hear our prayers.

No one can have a heart in one condition and produce fruit of an opposite condition. The condition of your heart will affect your actions, and your actions will reflect your heart.

A PURE HEART

Tom knew he wanted to propose to his girlfriend, but there was one problem. He didn't have a ring, and he didn't know anything about diamonds. Tom soon learned that a large diamond could cost the same as some small ones. The difference was quality. Some of the larger diamonds looked perfect, but to a trained eye, flaws appeared. Tom had to decide whether to impress others or pay as much for a smaller, unflawed stone. He chose the purer stone that reflected his feelings for his bride-to-be.

Pure means "to be singular in substance, without any imperfections or impurities." A pure heart is one solely committed to Christ first and foremost (Matt. 10:37–39).

"Blessed are the pure in heart, for they will see God" (Matt. 5:8). The word *sincere* is closely associated with purity. It comes from the Latin phrase *sine cere* meaning "without wax." Wax was often used to cover or fill in cracks in pottery so that it could then be sold as undamaged. Under the test of fire, the wax would melt and reveal the otherwise hidden cracks and impurities. If we want God to reveal himself to us so we can see him clearly, we must approach him with "clean hands and a pure heart" (Ps. 24:4).

"Do not consider his appearance or his height, for I have rejected him. The LORD does not look at the things man looks at. Man looks at the outward appearance, but the LORD looks at the heart" (1 Sam. 16:7). The pure in heart are precious gems of great value to God.

A CONTRITE HEART

Contrite means to be "humble and repentant before God,"[2] crushed by a sense of guilt and sin. In one way we are responsible for how we come before God. In another way, God will bring us to the edge of brokenness through our circumstances. Part of a covenant love relationship involves God's helping us to repent when we need to, but it still remains an act of our will. The prodigal son was not prevented from leaving the security of his father's house (Luke 15:11–32). His father allowed him the freedom to choose. But after the son came to the humiliating realization of where his decisions had led him, he repented and humbly returned to his father to ask forgiveness. His father ran to meet him, rejoicing in his return.

Psalm 34:18 says,

> "The LORD is near to those who have a broken heart,
>   And saves such as have a contrite spirit."
>
> (NKJV)

God can take a heart once hardened and rebellious and use circumstances to make it moldable and submissive. Without brokenness we become indifferent to God and to the needs of others. A proud heart exalts self and promotes independence from God. This is sin.

The result of a heart broken over sin is clear in Psalm 51:16–17:

> "For You do not desire sacrifice, or else I would give it;
>   You do not delight in burnt offering.
> The sacrifices of God are a broken spirit,
>   a broken and a contrite heart.
> These, O God, You will not despise."
>
> (Ps. 51:16–17 NKJV)

The remedy for sin is clearly repentence. David's heart cry, found in Psalm 51, still describes what men today feel when they repent of their sin and ask God to revive and refresh their relationship with him.

> "Have mercy on me, O God,
>   according to your unfailing love;
> according to your great compassion
>   blot out my transgressions.

Wash away all my iniquity
 and cleanse me from my sin....
Create in me a pure heart, O God,
 and renew a steadfast spirit within me.
Do not cast me from your presence
 or take your Holy Spirit from me.
Restore to me the joy of your salvation
 and grant me a willing spirit, to sustain me."

(Ps. 51:1–2, 10–12)

FEAR OF GOD

Fear brings a sense of awe and reverence toward God. Sometimes biblical fear can also refer to terror or dread when facing God's judgment. A lack of fear of God demonstrates a lack of understanding of who God is and what he is able to do.

Christians display a lack of fear when they

- ▸ continually use God's name in vain;
- ▸ deliberately sin, expecting God to forgive them;
- ▸ view worship, prayer, tithing, studying God's Word, and commitment to the church as options for the Christian;
- ▸ approach God in worship with a flippant attitude.

The apostle Paul knew God. The same man who wrote of the unfathomable depths of God's love in Ephesians 3 spoke of "the terror of the Lord" in 2 Corinthians 5:11 (NKJV). His certainty of God's judgment motivated him to persuade others of the truth. Fearing God is part of walking in his ways, loving him and serving him with all our hearts as we observe his commands. "And now, O Israel, what does the LORD your God ask of you but to fear the LORD your God, to walk in all his ways, to love him, to serve the LORD your God with all your heart and with all your soul, and to observe the LORD's commands and decrees that I am giving you today for your own good?" (Deut. 10:12–13).

Too often we are more afraid of men than we are of God. Most men dread being ridiculed by others. Jesus warned, "'Do not be afraid of those who kill the body but cannot kill the soul. Rather, be afraid of the One who can destroy both soul and body in hell'" (Matt. 10:28).

Similarly, binding Satan, casting him out, and rebuking him are common in the prayers of some Christians. Christ was never pre-occupied with the satanic. Jesus knew that Satan had no power over him. Jesus declared, "'I saw Satan fall like lightening from heaven. I have given you authority to trample on snakes and scorpions and to overcome all the power of the enemy; nothing will harm you. However, do not rejoice that the spirits submit to you, but rejoice that your names are written in heaven'" (Luke 10:18–20). Satan was rendered powerless as the disciples stepped forth in obedience to the task Christ had given them. We must be wise to Satan's methods, but fear is to be reserved for the one who has the rights to our lives.

FAITHFULNESS

The word faithful is linked to a promise: "Be faithful, even to the point of death, and I will give you the crown of life" (Rev. 2:10). Faithfulness is a lifelong goal. It is persevering to the end. Faithfulness is remaining true to the Lord and his Word through discouragement and difficulty as well as joy and success.

Anything short of finishing the race is to be disqualified, and everyone who crosses the finish line is a winner.

> FAITHFUL—"STEADFAST, DEDICATED, DEPENDABLE
> AND WORTHY OF TRUST"[3]

Steve Eason was a Christian working in a country closed to Christianity. Yet, during his time there, he and his wife accepted opportunities to start Bible studies, share their testimonies, and bring the gospel to waiting hearts.

When government officials became suspicious of Steve, they searched his house for any sign that he was actively seeking to influence others with his faith. Miraculously, they overlooked all of his Christian materials—even those in plain sight. Eventually, Steve was deported—on the grounds that people around him were being changed!

God is searching for faithful men. He is searching for men he can trust to intercede on behalf of our nation. God is looking for men he can trust with God-sized tasks (Ezek. 22:30). Will you be that man? Will his eyes rest on you or pass over you?

You may have been unfaithful. You may have stumbled in the race and are limping along the sidelines. Forgiveness and restoration are available for those who recognize their failures and repent of them.

The eyes of Christ fell on his disciple Peter at a time of Peter's unfaithfulness. Peter ran out weeping bitterly because he recognized his own disloyalty (Luke 22:60–62). But Christ knew Peter's heart, and his eyes rested once again on Peter after the resurrection. Repentant Peter was forgiven, restored, and commissioned by his Lord (John 21:15–19).

A life of faithfulness begins with the first step of obedience and continues one step at a time. "Whoever can be trusted with very little can also be trusted with much, and whoever is dishonest with very little will also be dishonest with much" (Luke 16:10). Measure your faithfulness by applying this principle to your faithfulness to your family, friends, self, and employer. You will find it harder to be faithful to God if faithfulness is not a part of what you are in your other relationships.

> "Be faithful, even to the point of death, and I
> will give you the crown of life."
>
> (Rev. 2:10)

OBEDIENCE

The apostle John wrote, "This is love for God: to obey his commands. And his commands are not burdensome" (1 John 5:3). Many have rightly said that it is impossible for a man who loves God to say, "No, Lord," because if Christ is truly our Lord, we cannot refuse him.

Obedience is submission to the instructions of an authority. Our obedience to Christ's commands is proof to God and to everyone watching us that Christ indeed is Lord of our lives. The act of baptism for a new Christian is the first act of obedience in response to the commands of Jesus Christ.

"To obey is better than sacrifice" (1 Sam. 15:22). God doesn't want you just to give more money to the church. God isn't looking to see how many hours you spent witnessing. It doesn't really matter how much you feel you had to give up to follow Christ. God wants to see if you have truly heard him. He wants to see you obey.

Luke 6:46 contains Jesus' question, "Why do you call me 'Lord, Lord,' and do not do what I say?" Before we decide he was talking to someone else, we must think carefully over the past few weeks. Has God told us to do some things that we have not done? Is the obedience response a normal part of our lives? God loves obedience.

SEEKS AND LOVES GOD

God's Word says, "Do not worship any other god, for the LORD, whose name is Jealous, is a jealous God" (Exod. 34:14). God not only demands our complete loyalty, but he also deserves it. God desires to be found by those who are seeking him. God longs to reveal himself to his people and share the blessings he has waiting for us. Even more, God wants to commune with us in a reciprocating love relationship.

Another paradox in the Christian life is that we must seek God with our whole heart in order to find him, yet it is God who causes us to want to seek him in the first place. Jeremiah 29:11–12 describes the special relationship and promise God has provided for us. "'For I know the plans I have for you,' declares the LORD, 'plans to prosper you and not to harm you, plans to give you hope and a future. Then you will call upon me and come and pray to me, and I will listen to you.'"

God sets in motion his plans and his purposes for you, then you will find in your heart a desire to seek after him. "'No one can come to me unless the Father who sent me draws him'" (John

6:44). It sounds so simple because it is, and yet all the complexity of God surrounds and enfolds that relationship. Love is the key. "We love [God] because he first loved us. If anyone says, 'I love God,' yet hates his brother, he is a liar. . . . Whoever loves God must also love his brother" (1 John 4:19–21). God's love leaves no room for hatred of anyone. God loves them, too, and we cannot love God and hate the very ones he loves.

It is easier for us to love those whom God loves if we allow God to love through us.. However, if we are disobedient, if we are choosing to serve ourselves and our biases against others, then we are divided. "No servant can serve two masters. Either he will hate the one and love the other, or he will be devoted to the one and despise the other" (Luke 16:13). Not only is it difficult, but resentment is bound to set in as the servant fails to serve either one adequately. Where does your devotion lie?

SERVANT OF THE LORD

We must remember that our commander-in-chief is Christ Jesus our Lord. God has placed us in situations according to his will and his purposes. In other words, we don't wait to see how our employer treats us before deciding how hard to work. Rather, we work as if Christ were our overseer, and in reality he is. God places us where he wants us to make a difference as his servants. "Whatever you do, work at it with all your heart, as working for the Lord, not for men, since you know that you will receive an inheritance from the Lord as a reward. It is the Lord Christ you are serving" (Col. 3:23–24).

Bob seemed ordinary enough. That is, until he began to speak. He shared how he had made his life available to God and the miraculous events with which God had involved him and the Christian men's organization he heads. Airlifts of blankets to refugees, semitrailers of supplies to tornado-ravaged locations, soup kitchens mobilized to flood disasters—on and on Bob shared how he had watched God match his people's resources with needs around the world.

Bob is a conduit through whom God's love flows to many nations. Bob's activities seem far removed from most people, but God found him faithful in small things and was able to trust him with more important tasks like the witness of lifesaving measures.

Whether we recognize it, God is involved in every aspect of our lives. He will take the ordinary circumstances we face and use them to develop our character. But our hearts have to be right first. If our hearts are sick or divided, we will view circumstances differently.

People commonly blame God for difficult situations or criticize him for his apparent lack of concern and involvement in our lives. However, God will use our circumstances for our benefit to promote greater dependence on him. God wants us to see how he works through challenging situations to overpower the evil one and to bring victory to those who love him.

Romans 8:28 is a promise of God. "We know that in all things God works for the good of those who love him, who have been called according to his purpose." God works for the good of those who love him. Our role is to be obedient to God and faithful as each task or circumstance is placed before us.

A HEART FOR GOD'S USE

The Bible offers guidelines to take us through life, like a plumb line builders use to see if a wall is perfectly straight (Amos 7:7–8).

Look at the following examples from God's Word and line your life up against them to see if you have moved away from "plumb" or being perfectly straight. If a wall is no longer straight, the foundation, rather than the wall, may have shifted. The foundation of a Christian life is a love relationship with God.

SET YOUR HEART TO FOLLOW GOD

"Set your heart" (2 Chron. 11:16) means to make following God your number-one priority. Nothing else can be more important to you than following God in every area of your life. Nothing else can take first place in your life. That position must be reserved for the one who can put everything in perspective. "'Any of you who does not give up everything he has cannot be my disciple'" (Luke 14:33).

Joseph had the responsibility of his young bride Mary and a newborn baby. It was crucial for him to have a heart that leaned toward God. God spoke to Joseph in a dream about the danger Herod had planned. At that point, Joseph's obedience determined whether his son would have a future. It is just as true today. Fathers, your obedience to God influences the future of your children.

YIELD YOUR HEART TO GOD

"'Now then,' said Joshua, 'throw away the foreign gods that are among you and yield your hearts to the LORD, the God of Israel'" (Josh. 24:23). *Yield* is translated in other versions as *incline* or *be always leaning in God's direction*. A friend who served as a campus student ministries director told his student council that there would be no excuse good enough for missing council meetings. Even in the case of death they had to be found pointing in the direction of the student building. In a humorous manner he made his expectations of loyalty and commitment clear. Our first and immediate inclination in any situation must be toward God and his standards.

CLEANSE YOUR HEART FOR GOD

The prophet Samuel instructed his people who were in great peril. "'If you are returning to the LORD with all your hearts, then rid yourselves of the foreign gods ... and commit yourselves to the LORD and serve him only, and he will deliver you'" (1 Sam. 7:3–4).

To commit our hearts to God we must give up those things in our lives that have given us "heart trouble." Even a hint of these things remaining in our lives can lead to major heart trouble. When we see words like *anything* and *everything* and *all* in Philippians 4:6–7, we can begin to see how thorough God intends to be in cleansing us for his use. "Do not be anxious about anything, but in everything, by prayer and petition, with thanksgiving, present your requests to God. And the peace of God, which transcends all understanding, will guard your hearts and your minds in Christ Jesus" (Phil. 4:6–7).

From what do you think the peace of God should guard your heart? How much better off would you be spiritually? The list could include greed, impure thoughts, hatred, and sexual immorality. Do you see the contrast between those things and the peace of God? God will help us be cleansed when we turn loose of dissension, discord, rage, and envy, and instead make those things that are really getting us into requests we give to

God. His peace will take the place of those anxieties while he responds to our prayers.

God calls these the "deeds of the flesh" or the "acts of the sinful nature." "Those who live like this will not inherit the kingdom of God. . . . Those who belong to Christ Jesus have crucified the sinful nature with its passions and desires. Since we live by the Spirit, let us keep in step with the Spirit" (Gal. 5:21, 24–25).

GUARD YOUR HEART

When Jesus was asked which of the commandments was the greatest or most important to keep, he said, "" Love the Lord your God with all your heart and with all your soul and with all your mind"" (Matt. 22:37). Your heart is the key to your relationship to God.

> "Above all else, guard your heart,
>   for it is the wellspring of life."
>
>   (Prov. 4:23)

You can determine to guard your heart against those things that would diminish your devotion to God. You can decide not to be put into compromising situations that would call into question your determination to serve God or cause your character to be suspect. You can place around you things to remind you of your love and commitment to God and ask fellow Christians to hold you accountable in your relationship to God (Job 1:10). You can refuse to give in to the temptations which follow closely behind you.

Guarding your heart means to put a hedge of protection around it because it is "the wellspring of life," the source of life-giving water.

DO NOT HARDEN YOUR HEART

"'Today, if you hear his voice, do not harden your hearts'" (Heb. 3:8). Hardhearted people are often associated in the Bible with being "stiff-necked" (2 Chron. 36:13). These terms describe a people who will not bow their heads to God and who live in willful rebellion against him.

Hardening of the arteries results from a buildup of fatty material on the artery walls. It restricts blood flow from the heart, often leading to heart attack, stroke, or damaged organs. Just as hardened tissues can cause great peril to your body physically, so a hardened heart can bring great harm to your spiritual life. Rebellion, pride, independence, anger, resentment, and bitterness can cause your heart to harden.

There is a cure. God alone has the cure to soften a hardened heart: repentance and release of our lives into God's hands. God says, "'I will give them an undivided heart and put a new spirit in them; I will remove from them their heart of stone and give them a heart of flesh. Then they will follow my decrees and be careful to keep my laws. They will be my people, and I will be their God'" (Ezek. 11:19–20).

TIME OUT!

Let's stop at this point and take a breath. You may be asking, "Who possibly could meet up to this God-sized challenge?" I mean, if you ever met a man who met the entire criterion, you might not feel worthy to walk in his footsteps! That's the point. We really are not worthy, because the only one who truly matches this criterion is Jesus Christ. But Christ in us can make the impossible possible. The Bible commands us to put on Christ. "All of you who were baptized into Christ have clothed yourselves with Christ" (Gal. 3:27). We are to clothe ourselves with Christ. "Rather, clothe yourselves with the Lord Jesus Christ, and do not think about how to gratify the desires of the sinful nature" (Rom. 13:14). God has also provided for us to become like Christ. "For those God foreknew he also predestined to be conformed to the likeness of his Son, that he might be the firstborn among many brothers" (Rom. 8:29). These are hefty commands!

These commands are God's strategy, his method to help us experience the full and abundant life Christ has to offer. "It is God who works in you to will and to act according to his good purpose" (Phil. 2:13). God knows we are flawed creatures because of sin. In reality, most of the great men God used had major character flaws. From Adam to Abraham, from Moses to David, each one demonstrated how frail humanity is. With the indwelling of the Holy Spirit, our will comes into line with Christ's will; our purposes begin to parallel his.

Our hands, feet, and mouths become God's tools to touch people we meet day after day. We begin to see God working in the lives of those we thought were hopelessly doomed. We begin to see people as Christ sees them, their needs, their spiritual hunger, their emptiness filled with worldly imitations of God's truth.

"Now to him who is able to do immeasurably more than all we ask or imagine, according to his power that is at work within us, to him be glory in the church and in Christ Jesus throughout all generations" (Eph. 3:20–21).

Each of us must begin where he is. We can't just jump into perfection or completion in Christ. God looks at our hearts and at the direction we are headed. If we set our hearts on God, he will set his heart on us. His role is to bring us to completion; our role is to let him and to cooperate with him.

Philippians 2:12–13 states this paradox: "Continue to work out your salvation with fear and trembling [your part], for it is God who works in you [his part] to will and to act according to his good purpose."

THINK ABOUT—PRAY ABOUT

God is in the process of making the ordinary extraordinary. If you are willing to let him take your life as a potter takes clay, you are already underway in an exciting journey with Almighty God!

▸ Think of two people in your life who show consistency between their actions and inner convictions. Now think about your own character. Do you show consistency between your actions and your convictions at home? at work? in private?

▸ Acts 13:22 says, "'I have found David son of Jesse a man after my own heart; he will do everything I want him to do.'" Are you willing to do everything God wants you to do? Pray about your willingness to become a man after God's own heart.

▶ Not calling for justice is equal to giving birth to evil. We know God has said in his Word that the result of sin is always the same, even if it is explained or justified by men.

▶ As leaders in our homes, churches, and workplaces, we must fear God. We should root out anything that dishonors God or would lead others astray. We may face permanent consequences if we continue to sin. The fear of God produces holiness in our lives.

▶ The Holy Spirit is seeking to empower you to want to do his will. Cooperate with him to change you, mold you, and prepare you for his will for your life. Those who resist, quench, grieve, or put off the Spirit will do so at the cost of their relationship with God. To resist the prompting of the Spirit in your life is to say you have lost your love for God. Meditate on this verse, "'If you love me, you will obey what I command'" (John 14:15).

Take a moment to thank God right now for his love and his care for your life.

---

1. Fernando Hernandez, "It's a Challenge," *Experiencing God Report* (July 1996), 6.
2. *Holman Bible Dictionary* (Nashville: Holman Bible Publishers, 1991), 293.
3. Ibid., 470.

Chapter 2

How God Shapes a Man

"I know the plans I have for you," declares the LORD,
"plans to prosper you and not to harm you,
plans to give you hope and a future."

—Jeremiah 29:11

Trouble! Throughout the Bible, God often used trouble to shape, grow, and discipline his people. Today, most of us would readily admit we are shaped by our experiences. God has provided us that characteristic so he can shape us. Each life experience, enjoyable or not, can remind us of our dependence on God. He is the source of every good thing, as well as the one who strengthens, guides, and helps us in times of trouble.

God is certainly able to shape a man through blessings. The life of Job was one of many blessings that nevertheless grew a character in him that continued to trust God, even when tragedy left him with nothing else. More often, however, men learn only when they are in trouble that God alone is able to handle all they face. In times of serious crisis men realize their dependence on God's love. Even so, God can use every day and every circumstance to teach and deliver us. As God does, he shapes us to make us more useful to himself.

GOD'S PLAN

The biblical story of Moses is one that has captured my imagination throughout the years. I remember some years ago watching the movie *The Ten Commandments*. I was awestruck by the actors and special effects portraying the drama and miracles of the events of Exodus. The four-hour epic passed quickly as I watched the Bible come alive.

For the real-life Moses, living through those events was another story. From his birth to his death 120 years later, Moses was molded and shaped by God through scores of circumstances. God searched for a man to fashion into an instrument to lead his people out of the bondage of slavery into freedom and into a new relationship with himself. God found Moses, a shepherd, a murderer on the run. Yet Moses was a man with a heart that sought God.

For us to understand how God shapes a man like Moses, we need to go back to his beginning, back to the Nile Valley. God placed Moses in unusual circumstances. Moses was trained by the best minds in Egypt. The adopted grandson of Pharaoh, he knew the workings of Pharaoh's court and the strategies of ruling a nation. God allowed Moses to grow up in a training ground and to gain insights that God would use for his glory forty years later.

God Uses Our Past to
Bring Glory to Himself

We all have unique personal histories. You may have had a relatively uneventful life, while others have endured many hardships. Some of you have emotional and physical scars from your past. Understandably, many men blame the past for their present troubles. However, God wants to use your past for his glory, both your successes and your failures. Romans 8:28 promises that God is working for the good of those who serve him, though this may not always be apparent to us at the time.

For instance, you may have grown up with circumstances you'd rather forget. How has God used the tragedies of your past to deepen your dependency on him? Do you understand that God walked with you through those trials to prepare you for a ministry to others?

The tragedies of life often force us to cry out to God. We watch as he takes our situation to bring glory to himself and blessings to us. It would be sad for you to hold bitterness against God and blame him for what you endured early in life. God loves you dearly and brought you through those trials so you can experience his deeper presence in your life. God spared you to have a life filled with joy in your salvation and to give you the purpose and meaning for which you may be searching. Are you consciously aware of the Father's loving you? He does love you. "God works for the good of those who love him, who have been called according to his purpose" (Rom. 8:28).

Don't think that your background is too rebellious, too difficult, or too sinful for God to use you. If you have been guilty of deceit, robbery, hatred, racism, adultery, murder, or rebellion, you are in the same company as Moses, David, Paul, Abraham, Jacob, and others.

God doesn't take you just the way you are. He takes you in spite of the way you are. He takes your willing heart, regardless of its past, and creates a new heart, one that seeks after God. When that happens, you will know it is God who is doing the work and not you.

God can use each life experience to shape a man. He can use experiences to equip us for ministry to others. God will bring circumstances to mind that will allow us to encourage others as we share how God was faithful through our struggles and victories. Each situation we face in life further develops our character.

Character is not only shaped by crisis; it is revealed in crisis. When crises occur, you can discover more about yourself as you listen to the words that come out of your mouth, as you see what actions you take, and as you monitor your attitude and evaluate how Christlike it is.

Life's circumstances teach us most about our character and God's faithfulness. God can use both our failures and our successes for his glory. He can take what we have done to ourselves and what others have done to us for his glory. Remember, "Where sin abounded, grace abounded much more" (Rom. 5:20 NKJV).

Nothing life brings your way is beyond God's ability to use for his purposes. Ephesians 2:10 declares that we are God's handiwork, born again through Jesus to do all the good things that God has planned for his kingdom. It probably is not hard to think of how God has taken something from someone else's past and used it to do a good work. It might be harder to imagine how our own past can be redeemed by God and used in the future. Moses makes a good case study for God's ability to shape men for his use.

Moses' Preparation

The first eighty years of Moses' life was a training ground for his future. He was a prince with a royal education and knew all the benefits of palace life. Then he became a fugitive on the run for murdering an Egyptian. Moses was exiled to the Sinai wilderness far from his family and home, tending goats and sheep. Regardless of how bleak his future may have seemed, he was where God wanted him—humble, moldable, and teachable.

God said, "'Like clay in the hand of the potter, so are you in my hand'" (Jer. 18:6). Moses' circumstances prepared him for a critical time in the history of God's people. Eighty years passed before Moses was ready to listen and obey God, eighty years before God used the lowly shepherd to bring the mighty Pharaoh to his knees.

God's Pattern for Using a Man

Scripture shows a pattern in the lives of the men God used. David, Moses, Abraham, Christ's disciples, Paul, and Gideon each experienced God's method for accomplishing his will through men.

▸ God chooses a man and makes plans for his life. "'You did not choose me, but I chose you and appointed you to go and bear fruit—fruit that will last'" (John 15:16).

▸ God issues a call to the man, an invitation to join him in touching a people in need.

▸ God prepares or fashions the man into the vessel that can best accomplish his will.

▸ God uses the man. In doing so, God actually prepares the man to be used again. Through the man's faithfulness God entrusts greater responsibilities.

God's pattern—choose, call, prepare, use—is demonstrated in the lives of Christ's disciples. At first glance, it appears that a motley crew of thrown-together, woebegone followers trailed after Jesus from town to town. But God had chosen each one from before the foundations of the world to be great for him.

Christ issued a call, "Come follow me." Some had been fishermen. Now they would be fishers of men. They would be shaped and molded through a three-year discipleship program with Jesus Christ as the distinguished professor.

Jesus taught his disciples to see the activity of the Father in the ordinary circumstances of life. Every situation revealed the Father's nature and his will to reach lost humanity: a lame beggar crying out for mercy on the side of the road, a widow mourning the loss of her only son, two blind men requesting healing for their eyes, a father protectively clinging to a possessed child, a prostitute anticipating her execution, four desperate men pleading for their friend to be healed. Christ used each one to teach the disciples how the love of God could change lives forever.

We are not called to a task, a mission, a job, or a ministry. We are called to a relationship with our heavenly Father. We become obedient to him in our activities, but we are called to a relationship.

Throughout life your call never changes, but your task or ministry focus may change many times. Jesus' call was to a relationship with the Father; Christ is our model in living this call.

Christ Is Our Primary Example

Christ is our primary example of how God uses a man in relationship to himself. The theme of the Bible can be summed up under two major points.

1. The Bible is the record of God's activity among men to bring them into a right relationship with himself.

2. The Bible is a demonstration of how we as Christians ought to live in relationship with the Father. This is shown in the two greatest commandments: to love God with all your heart and soul and mind; and to love your neighbor as yourself (Matt. 22:37—39). The importance of Christ in your life cannot be exaggerated.

Christ in your life means Christ is directing you, empowering you, and living through you. Nothing is impossible for you and Christ to do together. The key is the condition of your heart. If you truly love God with all your heart, you will be in right relationship with him.

The Christian life is Christ living out his life in you just as God lived through Christ. God's Word says that Christ is the key to living a godly life. In fact, Christ is the only way to live a godly life. The Bible tells us to dress ourselves in Christ (Rom. 13:14); to have Christ's attitude (Phil. 2:5); and to say and do everything we say and do in the name of the Lord Jesus Christ (Col. 3:17).

These are commands, so there is a difference between repeating them and doing them. Obedience can only be accomplished by doing what God has said. Christ must be visible in your life to those around you, in your attitudes, actions, and words. Ask yourself how the Father sees the situation, how his purpose could be served. Ask God to allow you to see those around you as the treasures he sacrificed his Son to save. Be like Jesus and allow the Father to speak through you.

RESULTS OF A SPIRIT-FILLED LIFE

Take a moment to meditate on this verse: "I have been crucified with Christ and I no longer live, but Christ lives in me. The life I live in the body, I live by faith in the Son of God, who loved me and gave himself for me" (Gal. 2:20).

What an amazing thought: Christ actually lives inside you and me! The Spirit of Christ takes up residence in our being as we commit our lives to him.

When anyone becomes a Christian, he dies to himself so that Christ can live through him (Col. 3:3). We are raised up to new life with Christ (Col. 3:1). We no longer live for ourselves but for Christ. We "continue to work out [our] salvation with fear and trembling, for it is God who works in [us] to will and to act according to his good purpose" (Phil. 2:12−13). When we are saved, we take into our lives all that God is—Father, Son, and Holy Spirit. The Spirit is given to teach and lead us into all truth (John 14:26; 16:13−15).

Christ's transforming presence changes our lives so that we can serve God. The Spirit helps us build godly character from the inside out. Godly character results in doing what is right even if we suffer for it (1 Pet. 2:20−23). Jesus gave his life for us. It is possible that we could be required to give our lives for him, or at least to patiently endure suffering for his sake. What kind of character does it take to do that? The character of Christ, the spiritual fruit that the Holy Spirit can produce in us when we follow God's commands (Gal. 5:22−23).

Testing Your Faith

God will test you to see what is in your heart. God's message to the Israelites as they came to the end of years of journeying toward the promised land was, "Remember how the LORD your God led you all the way in the desert these forty years, to humble you and to test you in order to know what was in your heart, whether or not you would keep his commands" (Deut. 8:2).

In another time and place David, the shepherd king of Israel, actually asked God to put him to the test.

> "Search me, O God, and know my heart;
> test me and know my anxious thoughts.
> See if there is any offensive way in me,
> and lead me in the way everlasting."
>
> (Ps. 139:23–24)

Salvation is more than going to heaven when you die. Eternal life is an intimate, personal, progressive relationship with the Almighty God and his Son. When salvation comes to your life, God radically and immediately reorients you for the rest of your life to Christ's right to be Lord.

On several occasions, God allowed my wife and me to get to the point where we feared we would sink financially. We had a crisis of belief. God waited to see if we were going to remain faithful to his promises to us or strike out on our own without him. We chose to cling to God's promises. We believed God was in control of our lives and our future.

Today our relationship with God is deeper and our marriage is stronger because of our obedience to him. We discovered how practical our relationship with God can be. We have watched

God affirm his love for us over and over in how he has taken care of us. We didn't sink. Instead, Christ helped us "walk on water" safely to the shore. An unexpected check would arrive in the mail, or one of God's people would leave an anonymous envelope with just the right amount of money to pay our bills. The unexpected money wasn't always a miracle, but the timing was! Just the right amount and just the right time. That's God!

God tests whom he chooses. Perhaps the ultimate test was given to Abraham when God asked him to give his only son as a sacrificial offering. Abraham revealed what was in his heart by his obedience, and God prevented his sacrificing his son. " 'Do not lay a hand on the boy,' [God] said. 'Do not do anything to him. Now I know that you fear God, because you have not withheld from me your son, your only son'" (Gen. 22:12).

As I toured the Apollo Space Program in California some years ago, I was struck by the meticulous way in which the space-craft was assembled. I was told that each piece was put under a stress tolerance test before it could become a part of the structure. Scientists deliberately stressed the parts beyond the levels they anticipated in case they had miscalculated their figures. Only after a part had endured testing would it be approved for assembly.

God places us in situations to test our level of faith. We will only be placed in the areas of ministry that we are able to handle. God tests us to see if our commitments are sincere. We often make commitments on a spiritual "mountaintop." But in living them out in the valley of everyday life, God will see if the commitment was real.

We need to be reminded of two important truths:

▸ We are in an ongoing love relationship with God.
▸ We were created for eternity.

When God encounters us, he does so out of love and for our best interests. He wants to fellowship with us and to partner with us to impact his world. In reality, this relationship is undeniably lopsided. God knows in advance what situations we will face. God knows just where and when he needs us to be a godly influence. He chooses and prepares us, equips and empowers us. Then God works in the outcomes to bring glory to himself. When we enter into a relationship with God and act in obedience to him, we impact eternity. God's primary activity today is to reconcile man to himself so man will not have to spend eternity separated from him.

"Consider it pure joy, my brothers, whenever you face trials of many kinds, because you know that the testing of your faith develops perseverance. Perseverance must finish its work so that you may be mature and complete, not lacking anything. . . . Blessed is the man who perseveres under trial, because when he has stood the test, he will receive the crown of life that God has promised to those who love him" (James 1:2—4, 12).

THE ROLE OF SCRIPTURE

Perhaps the easiest way to see how God works is through his inspired Word. When you sit down with the Bible and begin to read God's truth, the Holy Spirit may cause you to linger over a verse or two, or perhaps a certain phrase will catch your attention. Maybe something you read will stay with you throughout the day and you wonder what God wants to say to you.

The Bible says God will use Scripture to permeate our minds and speech (Heb. 4:12−13). Only when I spend time reading the Bible am I able to bring God's truth into conversation with others at their time of need. God also uses his Word as a reminder when I am tempted to do wrong.

As I teach the Bible to others, often I encounter someone with a differing viewpoint or a perspective that may not be biblical. God reminds me of 2 Timothy 2:24−25: "The Lord's servant must not quarrel; instead, he must be kind to everyone, able to teach, not resentful. Those who oppose him he must gently instruct, in the hope that God will grant them repentance leading them to a knowledge of the truth." Knowing this, I must temper my response with care and concern instead of trying to defend myself or my position.

BIBLICAL EXPECTATIONS

A particular verse or principle Christ taught in the Bible may guide us. Let's look at two examples. Matthew 25:21 tells us that God will give us a "few things" to see how we handle them. Then, if we are faithful, he will trust us with "many things." This is true in all areas of life.

Consider this principle applied to family life. When God gives a Christian man a spouse, he is commanded to love her as Christ loved the church and gave his life for the church. That is some kind of love! That kind of love will bring a loving response from a wife. If we are faithful in acting Christlike to our wives, God will bless our marriages with a deepened respect and love for each other. God may bless us with children. If we faithfully love, care for, discipline, train, and model for them what a Christlike father should be, God will build a bond between us and our children that he can bless. Faithfulness to God is always rewarded, regardless of whether it is in God-honoring relationships or in the way we use our time and possessions.

God has said that the devil will test our faithfulness, even to the point of death (Rev. 2:10). But even as God told early believers in part of what is now Turkey, the reward of faithfulness is the crown of life. Enduring suffering for Christ's sake is a witness to the truth of God. Ask yourself, "Would I trust God who gave me faith and eternal life to guide me through attacks by those who use fear and have no power over eternal life?" Consider the following:

In the seventeenth century, the government of Bern, Switzerland, enacted a law making it illegal for people to gather to pray or worship in groups larger than two, unless it was for a state-approved worship service. Melchior Brenneman was one of the Anabaptists who continued to gather and pray. Members of Brethren groups, the Anabaptists, believed Jesus when he said that he is present where two or three are gathered together in his name (Matt. 18:20). To obey such a law and not gather would be to forbid Christ's presence among them.

Melchior was imprisoned for not obeying the law. Then he and other Anabaptists had their property confiscated and were exiled with their families to work the lands of rich men.

Melchior, his wife, and their five children remained faithful to God, despite persecution and years of forced labor. Decades passed, and Melchior died. Yet at least two of his children and their families were eventually able to flee persecution for the American colony of Pennsylvania. The faithfulness to God of one ordinary man set a spiritual course for his family and provided a godly heritage that still inspires descendants more than three hundred years later.[1]

BIBLICAL REQUIREMENTS

God not only has expectations for us, but he also has requirements in order for us rightly to be called Christians. God is searching for men of integrity to "stand … in the gap on behalf of the land so [He] would not have to destroy it" (Ezek. 22:30).

Will you be that man? Will you take your relationship with God seriously enough to purify your heart and renew your commitment to serve him without reservation? God is looking for men he can use to affect a world! Will his eyes rest upon you, or pass over you (2 Chron. 16:9)? Could future generations be affected by the story of your faithfulness to God?

BIBLICAL EXAMPLES

Let's look at a few of the men in the Bible whom God used and see how he took them from the ordinary, developed their character, and made them the extraordinary vessels he would use.

Abraham was called from his homeland to follow God to an undesignated place. Abraham was obedient to God and left his homeland, but he still had some character flaws that needed work. For one, Abraham was quick to deceive those in authority. God tested Abraham for years to determine where his loyalty was. By the time Abraham was told to offer his son Isaac as a sacrifice, he had experienced enough of God not to question him but simply to obey. Abraham was faithful and was rewarded. Not only did God bless him with possessions, but God also kept his promise and made Abraham the father of a nation through his descendants.

Joseph began life as a spoiled child in a blended family. He was hated by his older half brothers, who were often incensed by his pride and cockiness. He was sold into slavery, accused of raping his employer's wife, and thrown into prison far from his home and family. Joseph was alone with no hope. Even though he had been rejected by everyone he knew, he remained faithful to God. God was molding Joseph into a vessel he would use to affect a host of nations. Joseph's integrity and godly character showed clearly through the false accusations, even in the jail cell. God took him from the pit of captivity to the throne room of the palace. Joseph went from being rejected by all to being a ruler of all. God never forgot Joseph, nor was God punishing him. God had to test Joseph and teach him to depend on God for his very life so that he could be trusted to rule a nation.

David, the man after God's own heart, began life as a shepherd boy. He fought many battles to protect his flock against wild beasts. Even as a youth he gave God the credit for his victories. David had a passion for God and an unwavering trust in God's strength. He demonstrated his trust in God in slaying Goliath, and he showed his fear of God by not killing his sworn adversary, King Saul, when he had opportunity to do so. No other man in the Bible has written so extensively in praise of God as David did in the Book of Psalms. David displayed his relationship with God before us with tremendous transparency, honesty, and integrity. Even when caught in sin, David truly repented, faced the consequences, and sought to restore his relationship with his heavenly Father. Despite David's life being extremely diverse, God used him to encourage countless generations.

Daniel is introduced in the Bible as a young man being taken captive from his home by ruthless invaders and being led off to Babylon. He could have blamed God for his hard times but instead honored God with his decisions. Daniel determined not to defile himself with unhealthy food and wine but honored God with his body and his mind. He found favor with his captors, who placed him in positions of great responsibility and leadership. Daniel's devotion to God and his good character were so exemplary that his enemies used it against him. He refused to bow down to other gods even at the threat of death and was rewarded by God.

Simon Peter was called to discipleship right out of his work-place. He quickly became a leader in Jesus' band of followers and was privileged to be one of the inner circle that Jesus trained more intensely. He went places with Jesus others were not permitted to go. He boldly stepped out of the boat and walked on water with his Lord. Simon Peter was a promising leader, but he still had character that needed molding and strengthening.

Christ knew that Peter's exuberance was shallow, but Jesus had great plans for Simon Peter. " 'Simon, Simon, Satan has asked to sift you as wheat. But I have prayed for you, Simon, that your faith may not fail. And when you have turned back, strengthen your brothers'" (Luke 22:31–32). The faith Peter exhibited in Christ was the foundation upon which Christ built his church (Matt. 16:18).

How to Know When God Is Speaking to You

We are a people of the Book. The purpose of the Book, the Bible, is to reveal God and his ways. So, if you desire to know how God wants to relate to you, look into the Word of God.

Most Christians seem to be disoriented to God's Word. Either they are unfamiliar with what it says, or they don't know what to do with it. I have found during my ministry that Christians have gone from having the Bible as the only book to having it as a reference book to other Christian literature. Men read all about God and all about the Bible but rarely look in the Bible itself.

We don't know how to take the God who reveals himself through his Word and relate his Word to our daily lives. The essence of the Christian life is a personal relationship with a living Christ. If we do not know when God is trying to relate to us or when he is speaking through his Word, we are in serious trouble at the very heart of our Christian lives.

All it takes to appreciate light is trying to go somewhere in the dark. Walking even a short distance into the unknown carries the risk that the smallest bump, unexpected, can make us fall. Likewise, even the smoothest, widest path can't help us if we can't find it.

Psalm 119:105 says that God's Word is the remedy for the darkness. The alternative to viewing God's Word as "a light for my path" is to move toward a religion where we follow concepts and principles rather than a person. True Christianity is a love relationship with a living Person.

When I was courting my wife-to-be from four hundred miles away, she sent her picture and regularly wrote to me. I would sit at my desk in front of her picture and thoroughly read her letter. Tingles would come all over me. As wonderful as it was to have her letters, I would have far rather had her sitting beside me.

We have a picture and a letter from God. His letter is designed to lead us to him. Knowing about God is different from knowing

God. The letter is lifeless and powerless without the living presence of God to go with it.

All of the Old Testament says God spoke. Sometimes he spoke through a vision or through angels. Other times he used a burning bush, handwriting on a wall, or an audible voice. How God spoke is not so important as the fact that he spoke. Every person in the Bible who encountered God knew when God was speaking and knew exactly what God said.

God is not predisposed to playing guessing games. We cannot say, "God bless me if my decision is right and stop me if it is wrong." I challenge you to find a place in the Bible where God says, "I'll hide my will from you, and you guess what it is! I'll bless you (or open doors) if your guess is right and stop you (or close doors) if you are wrong." God communicates through his relationship with us. If our relationship is not what it should be, we will not hear God.

Only Moses encountered God at a burning bush. Paul didn't have a "burning bush" experience; neither did Abraham, Peter, or David. The method of communication is not important, but the relationship is. Joshua conquered many cities, but only once did he bring down the walls by marching and blowing trumpets. If the method were important, every city would have come down the same way. It wasn't the method; it was God.

If you want to know what God's will is for you or for your church, build a relationship with the one who knows. God will uniquely show you what he wants to do through you, and you will know it is not the method, but God. Too often we do all we can through programs or a method yet never experience what God could have done.

God doesn't bless programs—God blesses people. Men today are in danger of following a God they read about and hear about but never actually know personally. When God encounters a man, he reveals something that is God-like and God-sized. Too often we reduce our lives and futures down to what we can handle. When you start to listen to God, you will hear him tell you that he is about to do the impossible. And when you obey him, you will experience what he said to you.

You may be able to understand this practically if you look at your budget. Your budget will usually reflect what you believe about God. Do you obey God's Word and give at least 10 percent of your income to God? Many people have told me they can't afford to give money to God. That tells me more about what they believe about God than the state of their finances.

God does not need your money; he needs your obedience. If you can be trusted with a little, God can trust you with much.

I saw a church take this seriously as they planned their annual budget. They decided to scrap their usual method of preparing a budget and instead sat down and wrote out everything they sensed God telling them he wanted to do through their little church. Their budget went from $74,000 to $184,000 by the time they were through. They knew they could only manage the $74,000 and determined to watch, pray, and see how God would provide the rest. Then they went ahead by faith in the God who asked for their obedience. By the end of the year, they had $189,000 come through their budget! God was faithful as the church was obedient.

I worked with an association of churches whose income was $9,000 the previous year. When the World's Fair was held in our city, we set out to determine how God wanted us to impact the

World's Fair with his gospel. We set a budget of $210,000. We felt that we as churches would be able to manage $26,000 of that amount. We added what others told us they would help us do and then left the remainder to God. By the end of the first six months, we had received and spent close to $200,000!

> EVERY PERSON IN THE BIBLE WHO ENCOUNTERED
> GOD KNEW IT WAS GOD SPEAKING TO THEM AND
> KNEW EXACTLY WHAT GOD SAID TO THEM.

I am bothered when I hear the people of God say, "I don't believe God would have us do something we couldn't do ourselves. It just doesn't seem practical." Do you realize that God never told men to do something they could do on their own? The way you know God is in something is that it will be impossible for you to do it on your own. God wants to reveal himself to you through it all and increase your faith in him. When the Red Sea parted, was that practical? When manna fell from heaven, was that practical? When Lazarus was raised to life, the storm ceased, the blind were healed, and Christ was crucified, were those practical?

Don't relegate God to the spiritual and believers to the practical. The most practical thing in the life of a Christian is the presence of a living God. He is our life! How sad it is when the people of God don't believe God makes a practical difference in their lives. Don't reduce God to what you can do and then ask him to bless you.

The Spirit of God can do three things that no one else can do:

- ▸ Reveal truth to you.
- ▸ Teach you through Scripture. God will reveal himself and his ways to you through the Bible so you can adjust your life to what he has told you.
- ▸ Convict you of sin in your life.

When you open the Word of God and you know that only the Holy Spirit can give you understanding and reveal truth to you, don't say, "I had a wonderful truth revealed to me today when I was reading, and I sure hope this leads me to an experience with God." That *was* the experience with God.

When you realize that you can't understand the Word of God apart from the Spirit's revealing it to you, then you will realize that God has just encountered you. God will reveal himself to you from his Word so that you can immediately experience him just as he revealed it to you. Anything in your character that prevents you from fulfilling the role God has for you will be brought to your attention by the Holy Spirit.

THE ROLE OF PRAYER

Have you ever been at a place in your walk with God where you prayed, felt nothing was happening, and sensed dead silence from God? I have.

I couldn't get any word from the Lord or any impression that God was speaking to me. I came from a church background that said if God refuses to speak to you there must be sin in your life. I went through my checklist and found nothing in my life that God pointed out as sin. So I approached God through his Word again. I came across John 11. Jesus deliberately delayed going to

Mary and Martha until after his friend Lazarus had died. Mary and Martha told Jesus that if he had been there their brother would not have died. Jesus told them that they knew he could heal their brother from sickness, but he delayed coming because he felt they were ready for a greater revelation of him. They knew he was the healer; now they would see him as the resurrection and the life.

I went from depression to elation! I discovered that heaven wasn't closed because God was punishing me. Rather, God was preparing me for a greater blessing. I began to look around for what God was about to do in my life. I still go through the checklist to see if sin is the reason for God's silence. If it's not, then my concern turns to anticipation for what God is about to reveal to me about himself.

Martha was afraid of what they might find when her brother's tomb was opened. She may have also feared that her hopes for what Jesus could do would end in disappointment. But Jesus told her that, if she believed, she would see the glory of God (John 11:40).

If you believe in the Son of God for your salvation, search your life for something (worry, doubt, fears) that may be keeping you from seeing God's glory about to be revealed.

If you are prepared to anticipate God's activity, ask him to remove those worries, doubts, or fears.

LOVE EQUALS OBEDIENCE

Often when I am bringing my concerns before the Lord through prayer, he will impress a passage of Scripture on my mind. I may not know the reference, but I seek it out with a concordance until I find it. Men, prayer is interactive when you are in relationship with God. Some men feel they can't concentrate when they are praying because their minds begin to be filled with Scripture. This is God speaking to you. His Word is living and active. If you are always looking for God to answer your prayer, allow him to speak in any way he chooses.

The greatest proof of God's activity in the Bible is not just in the miracles but in the timing of the miraculous. You may scientifically explain how the Jordan River was backed up miles upriver by some quirk of nature. But you will have quite a time explaining how it happened at the precise moment the foot of the priest touched the water.

> ### God never told men to do something they could do on their own.

God intervened in the lives of his people over and over again as they prayed to him and waited for his response. When God says he is going to do something, what happens next is God. If you expect God to answer your prayers, then look around and see if your life is not in agreement with what God has revealed to you. After all that God has revealed to you through his Word, through your circumstances, and through your relationship with him, the bottom line is always your obedience. John 14:15 says, paraphrased, "If you love me, anytime I speak, you will automatically obey me."

Jesus said we are to obey—not wrestle, not fight, not argue. Are you fussing with God about any aspect of your relationship with him? Is something in your relationship causing a struggle? If you have to fight with God every time he reveals his will to you, you might want to check what sort of love relationship you have with him. If you require that God prove four different ways that he is speaking to you, it may mean you don't understand what a love relationship with God means.

I've been married several decades. If my wife even hints that she would like me to do something special for her, I go out of my way to do it because I love her. That is the same type of relationship God wants us to have with him. Do you realize what happens when you obey God? Your obedience to the slightest word from God sets in motion the activity of God. He comes alongside you and opens to you, your family, and your church his mighty acts.

THINK ABOUT—PRAY ABOUT

Are you relating what God has done in your life to a ministry for which you feel he has prepared you? Pray for a better understanding of what that ministry is and what you need to do to respond to God's leadership.

▸ James 1:2—4, 12 is a passage about stress tolerance. "Consider it pure joy, my brothers, whenever you face trials of many kinds, because you know that the testing of your faith develops perseverance. Perseverance must finish its work so that you may be mature and complete, not lacking anything. . . . Blessed is the man who perseveres under trial, because when he has stood the test, he will receive the crown of life that God has promised to those who love him."

▶ Pray and thank God for his Word of instruction and explanation regarding trials and perseverance.

▶ Do you believe God can use you? Will you trust his Word to guide you? Thank God for Scripture, and pray for understanding and wisdom as you read and study his Word.

▶ You may have tried courses, radio programs, Christian clubs and organizations, or even church without experiencing a loving relationship with God. Don't go any further until you talk to your Father who has been waiting for you all this time.

▶ Don't bring the truth of God down to the level of your experience. Lift your experience to the level of the description of Christ in the Bible. Your experience, or lack of it, does not validate the character and nature of God. You may not be experiencing the truth of God's Word, but that does not cancel God's truth. Pray and ask God to bring you into the excitement of a meaningful relationship with him.

---

1. Albert H. Gerberich, *The Brenneman History* (Scottsdale, Penn.: Mennonite Publishing House, 1938), 1–3.

Chapter 3

GOD'S
REFINING PROCESS

*"You did not choose me, but I chose you and appointed you to go
and bear fruit—fruit that will last."*

—John 15:16

Sometimes people receiving awards say they owe their
accomplishment to someone in particular. That person
might be a spouse, a parent, or a mentor. However, in the
broader picture, we owe our entire lives, both now and forever, to
the one who redeemed us from sin and death.

Being born again is a personal encounter with the truth that
Christ has chosen us. We have not chosen and pursued him. As
the Scripture tells us, Christ first chose us, appointed us, and
instructs us to bear fruit that will last. The fruit we bear will be
everlasting because we are branches that gain our life source
from the vine, Jesus Christ.

CHARACTER DETERMINES USEFULNESS

Believers are not where they are by accident. They gain more of God's perspective when they grasp a sense of divine appointment. But when believers grasp that they have been created for a particular time and place, they must also realize that they will be faced with opportunities to trust and serve God. Not the least of these opportunities is the realization that believers are also created for unity with one another. Depending on Christ to guide and develop unity between believers may be one of life's greatest challenges.

My father was a businessman in a small community. If God put him in a place with no evangelical church, he believed he should start one.

My first recollection of church was of being in a dance hall with my father preaching and my mother playing the piano. My older brother served as usher, and my younger brother and I were the congregation. For eight months it was just the five of us, until we started a Sunday school. It was eight years before anyone would come as our pastor.

That church is now the largest, strongest evangelical church in that town. My father took seriously the Book of Acts, which tells how God scattered the church and those who had been scattered preached the Word wherever they went (Acts 8:4). Christ did not choose preachers to follow him. He called small businessmen and others. My father was a deacon, a layman, and a businessman, but he didn't use the excuse that he wasn't a "preacher." He was a servant of God, committed to sharing the good news of Christ wherever God placed him.

In ancient times, kinship brought specific obligations to care for and protect related parties. When people were not of the same clan, a covenant would be used to define a relationship, binding the parties to the promises they made to one another. Two descriptions of God's covenant with his people can be found in Deuteronomy 7:9 and 29:12–13. In these verses, God promised that the Israelites were his people and that he was their God. He called this his covenant of love.

When you give Christ rule over your life, when you are "born again," you enter into a covenant love relationship with God. All there is of God, including his Son and his Spirit, comes to live in you to begin shaping your character and cleansing your life of all that hinders you from being used in his kingdom. This covenant relationship is not only between you and God, but it is also between God and all of his people.

If you belong to God, you are part of a chosen people, a royal priesthood, and a holy nation of people belonging to God (1 Pet. 2:9–10). Being in a covenant love relationship with God means that you will love and serve him, praising him for calling you out of the darkness of sin and into the light of his transforming love.

The presence of God in his people put fear in the nations surrounding them. The nations were not afraid of the Israelites. They were afraid of the *God* of the Israelites. How many people tremble before the God that churches serve in their communities? The fear of God will not come upon the people outside the church before it comes upon the people inside the church.

Every time anyone in the Bible of any significance met God, great fear, awe, and trembling came upon them. We talk about standing in the presence of a Holy God, yet our response to him is unlike anyone who stood before him in the Scriptures

(Jer. 5:22). We must ask ourselves if we are confronting God in such a way that a holy sense of trembling comes over us. How can Christians proclaim a message of urgency while living a lifestyle of complacency? People will believe the message when it is delivered by a messenger whose life demonstrates that he knows God and takes God seriously.

If we are Christians, we have living in us all of God's provision for a broken world. Christ, living in us, will make a difference through us. If people around us are not being affected by Christ, we must consider whether there is sin in our lives hindering Christ. If so, this indicates a heart problem. Christ is not truly our Lord if he is not having his way in our lives. If we are Christians and no one's life is being changed because of our presence, we have an immediate need for repentance.

Are there people who are now a part of God's kingdom because you shared God's good news with them? Can you identify people God placed in your life to encourage you to persevere in your walk with God? Allow God to make you that person in someone else's life.

CHARACTER STUDIES

Let's look at several examples from the Bible of men whose usefulness was determined by their character.

Barnabas was known for his ability to encourage others. He was the sort of friend everyone likes to have around. He had been a priest from Cyprus who sold all he had and gave it to the newly formed church in Jerusalem. Barnabas took Paul, the new convert, to Antioch to disciple him and train him in the way of Christ (Acts 11). He and Paul, under the leadership of the Holy Spirit, made a radical decision to take the gospel to the non-Jews amid much criticism. His faithfulness and obedience brought the gospel to those who could take it to the ends of the earth. Later, Paul took Silas, and Barnabas took young John Mark as their partners in mission work. Mark became the first to write an account of the life of Christ and became a great encouragement to the apostle Paul during Paul's time in prison. Barnabas was a man God could use.

Nehemiah had a cushy government job, a good life, and respect in the community, but his heart was broken. His people lived in exile while Jerusalem and its temple lay in ruins back in his homeland. God offered him the job of rebuilding the temple and its city walls (Neh. 1—2). Not only was God pleased to help Nehemiah, but the king supplied unlimited building materials, written protection, and authority to build. Despite the constant threats of war and the grumbling of the broken people he was leading, Nehemiah believed God and persevered until he completed the project. His people had a temple in which to worship God and a safe city in which to live. God used Nehemiah to restore his people to a covenant love relationship with him. Nehemiah was a man God could use.

Joseph, husband to Mary the mother of Jesus, was chosen by God to raise and nurture his Son (Matt. 1:18—25). Joseph demonstrated incredible faith and trust in God as well as obedience in times of dire circumstances (Matt. 2:13). He was a tradesman, a carpenter. Joseph was a man of simple means whom God found trustworthy and faithful. What greater privilege could a man have than to be the earthly father to the Son of God! Joseph was a man God could use.

Timothy was a son from a mixed marriage. His mother was Jewish, and his father was Greek. In his world, Timothy would have faced the ridicule of insensitive people from both sides. His godly mother and grandmother raised him to have faith in God. Timothy heard about Jesus Christ and all he had done. As a young believer, Timothy went with the apostle Paul on missionary journeys where he could see the power of God demonstrated. It soon became apparent to the Christian community that Timothy was well qualified to lead them as pastor. Paul continued his mentoring relationship by writing two letters to Timothy (1 and 2 Tim.) and was a great encouragement and model for him. Timothy was a man God used.

> "DON'T LET ANYONE LOOK DOWN ON YOU BECAUSE YOU ARE YOUNG, BUT SET AN EXAMPLE FOR THE BELIEVERS IN SPEECH, IN LIFE, IN LOVE, IN FAITH AND IN PURITY. UNTIL I COME, DEVOTE YOURSELF TO THE PUBLIC READING OF SCRIPTURE, TO PREACHING AND TO TEACHING."
>
> 1 TIMOTHY 4:12–13

Paul's instructions to Timothy (1 Tim. 4:12–13) gave five ways to set an example for believers. These instructions remind us that when we consider spiritual disciplines we must go beyond times of Bible study. Our disciplined walk with Christ is to be continuous in our speech, our lives, in the love we show, and in our faith and purity—as well as in reading Scripture, preaching, and teaching.

Paul was a man with misdirected zeal until Christ intersected his life on the road to Damascus. He had to be molded and shaped before God could use him significantly. This preparation encompassed at least twelve years before Paul became an intentional missionary. God used Paul, perhaps more than any other man, to spread the gospel through the known world. Paul needed much preparation in his faith because he eventually endured much pain and torture at the hands of evil men. He was happy to suffer for Christ because of all Christ had suffered for him. Paul was a man God used in a great way.

SOME MEN GOD COULD NOT USE

God will not use some men. Let's explore several types of men God chooses not to use.

MEN WHO KNOW BEST

Some simply decide they know best and strike out on their own apart from God. They decide that if it is going to be done they will have to do it themselves. Their motto is: Don't just sit there—do something!

God does not follow us. God leads us. For a man to refuse to wait on God is sheer arrogance and pride. That man will encounter the same fate as King Saul, who defied God's commands and offered sacrifices himself instead of waiting for God's prophet, Samuel. As a result, the Spirit of God no longer guided or empowered Saul, nor did God protect him from the onslaught of the forces of evil.

King Saul met his end on a battlefield fighting a war apart from God's strength and guidance. The prophet Samuel spoke judgment to the king: "'You acted foolishly.' . . . 'You have not kept the command the LORD your God gave you; if you had, he would have established your kingdom over Israel for all time'" (1 Sam. 13:13).

Saul apparently thought he was justified in disobeying God. Saul saw his men scattering, the prophet was late, the enemy was regrouping, and he needed a blessing before it was too late. So the king, believing that now everything was up to him, disobeyed God's order to wait for the prophet Samuel to come and offer the sacrifice required to gain God's favor.

God had already promised to deliver Israel (1 Sam. 12:22) because they were his people. He had delivered them many times before. Yet Saul's belief that he had to *do* something, even in direct diobedience of God's command, carried a heavy price. God would have continued Saul's dynasty forever. Now God rejected him and his house in favor of one with a heart for God (1 Sam. 13:14). By doing what seemed humanly expedient, Saul cut himself off from God's best. There is no justification for disobeying God. God seeks men after his own heart who will obey him.

MEN WHO PUT LIMITS ON GOD

Other men try to put conditions on how God can use them. I've heard some say, "I know God wouldn't send me to a cold country. I just can't stand the cold." Or, "I couldn't leave my family to follow God in missions. It would break their hearts." Or, "My business is going so well right now. I couldn't give it up yet to follow God."

Whatever the reason, it boils down to the fact that Jesus Christ is not truly Lord of their lives. God does not have free access to use anyone with those attitudes. If you put limits on how God will use you, you will be used little, if at all. The man God uses abandons his life into the hands of God. This is the only way you will truly find fulfillment and meaning in life.

Jesus explained it this way. "'I tell you the truth, ... no one who has left home or wife or brothers or parents or children for the sake of the kingdom of God will fail to receive many times as much in this age and, in the age to come, eternal life'" (Luke 18:29–30).

Why would someone choose anything in this life over a heavenly reward? How could someone move from a self-centered perspective to God's perspective?

MEN WITH DIVIDED HEARTS

Luke 18:18–29 is the account of Jesus' confronting a young, rich man. At first glance, it seems that Jesus rebuffed this follower. A wealthy young man who had kept the law all his life was asking Jesus how to inherit eternal life. Looking more closely, we see that this man was not ready to give up all and follow Christ. Jesus looked into his heart and saw what was hindering him from following wholeheartedly. His heart was divided. He could not follow Christ with all of his heart, soul, mind, and strength while he still held allegiances to others. The young man seemed to want to follow Jesus but on his terms, not God's. Sadly, he could not be used by God.

MEN WHO WILL NOT LISTEN TO GOD

Some refuse to believe God when he speaks to them. They will not trust that God knows what is best. Often they will characterize themselves as the pragmatic, realistic, or practical ones of the group. One man described himself as the "doubting Thomas" of his church. I challenged him at that point and asked him if he was talking about Thomas before or after he met the risen Lord. God says, "If anyone would come after me, he must deny himself and take up his cross daily and follow me. For whoever wants to save his life will lose it, but whoever loses his life for me will save it" (Luke 9:23–24).

MEN WHO SHRINK GOD

We are all guilty of being God-shrinkers. J. B. Phillips wrote a book entitled *Your God Is Too Small*. We bring God down to our level in our minds and then tell him what to do! Too often Christians live in a world void of faith, a world limited by their own understanding and power. Their view of God is narrow, confined, and powerless. There is no victory, no life, no joy, and no power flowing through them. Somehow they are content with that sort of life. How sad to have so much available to them through the Holy Spirit and not access any of it. These men have become of no use to God.

Paul wrote of a man named Demas who was a follower of Christ (Col. 4:14). But because he loved the world, Demas deserted Paul in his hour of need. "Do your best to come to me quickly, for Demas, because he loved this world, has deserted me and has gone to Thessalonica" (2 Tim. 4:9–10).

Apparently the cares of the world, the deceitfulness of wealth, or the worries of life choked out Demas's commitment to Christ, and he fell away. Christ has harsh words for those who seem to grow up among Christians but do not persevere to the end. He continues to say, "'The Son of Man will send out his angels, and they will weed out of his kingdom everything that causes sin and all who do evil. They will throw them into the fiery furnace, where there will be weeping and gnashing of teeth. Then the righteous will shine like the sun in the kingdom of their Father. He who has ears, let him hear'" (Matt. 13:41–43).

I am concerned that teenagers today may be unable to look across their churches and find godly models to follow. They observe how men treat one another in business meetings. They know about their fathers' business practices. They see how men react to crisis times in the church, either in faith in God according to God's Word or according to their own fears and abilities. When teenage boys see their models functioning just as the world does, they will also act as the world acts. Teenagers need to see men model a covenant relationship with God. They need to see men God uses and watch how God blesses them for their faithful service to him.

Unfortunately, too often we see men who demonstrate otherwise. God calls us to be people among whom he can keep coming in his mighty presence.

WHOM HE LOVES HE CHASTENS

Take a moment to read John 15:1–8, 16. This passage troubles some people because they believe that if they are not witnessing or leading people to Christ they will be taken away from

Christ and thrown into the fires of hell. That is not what this passage is saying. Jesus says he chose us to bear fruit, fruit that will last.

We see four things in this passage:

▸ Some branches he takes away;
▸ Some branches he prunes;
▸ There are conditions for bearing fruit;
▸ There is accountability to the vinedresser.

Other Scripture passages can shed light on this truth. For example, the parable of the sower and the seed (Luke 8:1–15) provides another picture of the same truth. Some seeds grew up quickly but fell away or withered. These are the branches that are gathered and burned in the fire. Only one of the four sowings of seed bore any sort of fruit. These are the seeds that parallel what Christ says about abiding in the vine, "'If a man remains in me and I in him, he will bear much fruit'" (John 15:5).

Further help in understanding this truth may be found in 1 Corinthians 3:12–15: "If any man builds on this foundation using gold, silver, costly stones, wood, hay or straw, his work will be shown for what it is, because the Day will bring it to light. It will be revealed with fire, and the fire will test the quality of each man's work. If what he has built survives, he will receive his reward. If it is burned up, he will suffer loss; he himself will be saved, but only as one escaping through the flames."

I once moved into a home that had beautiful, lush rose bushes. In fact, my new neighbors let me know in short order that they expected me to look after those roses they so admired. I knew nothing about caring for roses. After reading and studying all my mind could take about roses, I became distressed. I learned that I had to show "tough love" to these beautiful plants. My inherited rose bushes had to be chopped up in the fall in order for them to produce a healthy crop of roses the next year. I apologetically snipped here and there, begging the bush to forgive me with each careful cut. When I was through, it looked pathetic and helpless. But the secret was in the healthy roots, not the branches. Sure enough, the next spring, life once again reappeared. Almost effortlessly, dozens of buds began appearing at the end of the lush, leafy green branches. The bush had grown even bigger than it was the year before!

Christ must cut out the things in our lives that hinder growth and prevent us from bearing fruit. Useless branches can sap nutrients from the healthy branches. They can slow or hinder growth. Although painful at the time, it will be well worth the operation in the long run.

THE DISCIPLINE OF GOD

Shaping comes first, then discipline comes during our being used of God. The discipline of God is not spiritual warfare. Its purpose is to bring greater dependency on God. If our hearts depart, we are no longer being obedient to God. God's discipline is meant to benefit us because He loves us. How would your life be different now if no one ever disciplined or trained you? Perhaps you have already experienced some consequences from an earlier lack of discipline.

Take a moment to read and reflect on Hebrews 12:5–6 and Revelation 3:19. It is crucial that you distinguish between spiritual warfare and the discipline of God. Not everything negative that happens to you is necessarily a satanic attack. Some may be God trying to bring you back on track spiritually.

> "My Son, do not make light of the Lord's discipline,
>   and do not lose heart when he rebukes you,
> because the Lord disciplines those he loves,
>   and he punishes everyone he accepts as a son."
>
> (Heb. 12:5–6)

> "'Those whom I love I rebuke and discipline. So be earnest, and repent.'"
>
> (Rev. 3:19)

The prevailing attitude in many churches today says that blessings come from God and crises come from Satan. In the Old Testament, God alone destroyed his people. Nothing was allowed to harm the children of God without his permission. Only when God lifted his hand of protection from his people did enemy forces gain the victory. It was a clear indictment against the religious leaders of Jesus' day when they undeniably saw the activity of God and attributed it to Satan. Jesus called it blasphemy against the Holy Spirit (Matt. 12:22–32).

SPIRITUAL WARFARE

You can distinguish spiritual warfare from the discipline of God. God disciplines his children because he loves them. The discipline of God brings life. The activity of Satan brings death. Your life is either being renewed by God or depleted by Satan.

Satan desires to drive a wedge between you and God, to draw you away from God's presence. God's aim is always to restore his people into a right relationship with him. God will discipline you in such a way as to drive you back to dependency on him. Satan will try to interrupt your usefulness to God. Is God currently using you in an effective way to bring people to him? Satan's desire is to thwart the effectiveness of those God is using and to undermine their relationships with God. If you are not currently involved in effective kingdom ministries, God may be trying to get your attention. Satan won't bother with those who are ineffective and useless to God. If you find that your situation is driving a wedge between you and God and that your relationship with him is increasingly ineffective and distant, then you may be facing spiritual warfare.

The Bible contains many examples of both spiritual warfare and the discipline of God. Elijah fought spiritual warfare on Mount Carmel. Despite his fear and perceived aloneness, he stood unwavering in his commitment to God and gained the victory. Jonah faced the judgment of God because of disobedience. But for the grace of God, he would have perished at sea. King Saul faced the discipline of God and lost his kingdom because of disobedience and pride. King David faced the discipline of God, lost the life of his infant son because of adultery and murder, and watched as his family unraveled before his eyes. Christ faced spiritual warfare often with possessed individuals and with the temptations of Satan, who tried to separate the Son from the Father. The apostle Paul faced spiritual warfare when he was in prison and abused by those opposed to his gospel message.

A pastor once confided to me that he had committed adultery and lost his family and his church. He asked me to pray that God would restore his ministry and his family. I have seen the damage pastors have caused to multitudes of Christians because of their sin and disobedience to God. I told him I would pray, rather, that God would discipline him and use him as a model to other pastors who were contemplating the same kind of sin. I told him I would pray his life would be a testimony to the seriousness of sin and the devastation it brings upon other people. I firmly believe that to whom much responsibility is given, much is accountable. Accepting a position of leadership among God's people is serious business.

Several men I know have used King David as an excuse for their own flagrant sin of adultery. They argue that David was a man after God's own heart, and God forgave David after he committed adultery. The truth is David experienced dire consequences for his immoral lifestyle. When he committed adultery and murder, David showed absolute disdain for the God who gave him his kingdom. Even after he fully repented, he faced a bleak future. The infant son born through adultery died. David's son committed incest with his half sister; another son ordered the death of his half brother; the sword of death never left his family; his own wives and children turned against him; he was not allowed to build the temple for God; and he had to face constant reminders that he had murdered the husband of a woman he wanted for himself. David's sin affected many generations of his descendants. Although forgiveness comes after repentance, the pain and responsibility for sin may remain for a lifetime.

God will allow Satan to test your resolve as a Christian. God is searching for those whom he can trust and whom he can use.

GOD REFINES FOR HOLINESS

God's discipline is like the "refiner's fire" spoken of in Malachi 3:2. Fire can be used to refine, or purify, as when silver or gold are heated in a furnace until impurities float to the top of the melted metal and are skimmed away. When God's discipline begins to purify you, holiness will become evident in several ways.

> "Who can endure the day of his coming? Who can stand when he appears? For he will be like a refiner's fire or a launderer's soap."
>
> (Mal. 3:2)

> REFINER'S FIRE—USED TO REFINE, OR PURIFY, SUCH AS SILVER OR GOLD BEING HEATED IN A FURNACE UNTIL IMPURITIES FLOAT TO THE TOP OF THE MELTED METAL AND ARE SKIMMED AWAY.

YOUR LIFE

As the Spirit does his work in your life, your character will begin to relinquish all the impurities that have hindered you from God's use. Like a pure diamond, you will brilliantly reflect Christ's light to all those around you. Even in times of failure, your life will demonstrate a dependency on God's grace and a willingness to face any consequences as long as your relationship to the Master is restored. Your view of sin and the hurt it causes God will increase with your love for God and your willingness to obey him. All those around you will begin to see God more and you less as your life gives testimony to his presence within you.

YOUR MARRIAGE

The Spirit's refining process will affect your marriage as well. Your union with your wife will be centered around Christ as your common Lord. You will understand what it is to love your wife as Christ loved the church and gave his life for it (Eph. 5:25). Your home will be a place where both the lost and believers are welcome. Your home will be like a refuge and a sanctuary for souls that are weary and thirsty. Your marriage and your home will reflect God's wisdom and grace to those around you. Your wife will develop a deeper trust and love for you as she sees your desire to honor her. Your commitment and love for your wife will deepen as your commitment and love for your Lord increase.

You may not realize how much God has invested in your marriage. Your marriage may be the result of hundreds of hours of prayers offered by friends and family, asking God to help you choose a spouse wisely so God could bless your marriage. God has put two lives together that he has been molding since birth to be a powerhouse of his activity. Are you and your wife allowing God to use you to impact those to whom you relate? God has a good reason for investing so much into your marriage. He wants his investment reinvested in your offspring, and that could well include the godly influence of your household upon others. Malachi 2:15 states that you, as a husband, are to guard your spirit and not break faith with the wife of your youth.

If the man God uses is married, he has a marriage that reflects the same kind of selfless love and faithful commitment God shows his people. God will honor and bless this relationship and use it to bring glory to him.

YOUR FAMILY

As God brings his refining process into your life, your relationship with your children will change. Some things only God can do in a family. God can transform relationships and link your heart with your children's hearts (Mal. 4:6) in a way that honors him. He can also do that between your heart and those of your parents. If they are no longer living, he can repair past griefs and bring the peace that comes from repentance and forgiveness. Trust God to heal any wounds you carry. Thank God for providing your parents to bring you into this world.

You may have tried your best as a father but never seemed to get where you wanted to be with your children. Children have such different personalities, and some of the things they do are just plain annoying. As God works in your life, he will place in you a love for your children and an ability to teach them and train them that you never had before. As you begin to decrease and God begins to increase in your life, your children will begin to see Christ in you and no longer see your old nature. God will begin to turn the hearts of your children toward you. That is significant. Many temptations can turn hearts toward the world. What better choice is there than to have children's hearts turned toward a godly father.

The Holy Spirit is not just a guide to those seeking to further the kingdom, but he is also the guide to the parent who needs wisdom and patience (James 1:5). God looks for godly seed which he can use to impact generations to come (Mal. 2:15). He is interested in your family's being healthy and whole. Throughout the Old Testament, God made covenants with men and their descendants who were yet to be born (Gen. 17:7; Ps. 37:25).

You may pass on your flaws to your children, but are you consciously passing on your faith as well? The instructions to fathers in the Bible largely center around passing on stories of God's faithfulness to the father and to his forefathers. Father, you have a chance to bring great blessings to your children, grandchildren, and their grandchildren.

You were not created for time, but for eternity! Your decisions will have eternal consequences. Place your recent family decisions alongside John 12:35–36. How do your decisions reflect your trust in the light that Christ brings to you and your family? Is Christ transforming relationships in and through your family?

YOUR WORKPLACE

Holiness can be both a blessing and a curse. It can be a blessing because God will honor your commitment to him, and he will use you in a mighty way on a daily basis. It can be a curse because your mere presence can bring out the worst in others. This was realized in the life of Christ. He lived in the constant care and protection of his Father because of his obedience and love. Yet those all around him were either attracted to him or repulsed by him, depending on the condition of their hearts. The religious leaders of the day eventually had him crucified, partly because he constantly made them aware of their emptiness, corruption, and self-seeking religious practices. The religious leaders, the most respected men of the day, were reduced to reviling, spiteful, plotting assassins simply because Jesus healed a man who was blind (John 9:13–34). As a follower of the Master, you will also experience both blessing and curse.

Your holiness will bring out the best and the worst in others (John 15:18–25). Your commitment to God will reveal their lack of commitment. Your love for God will reveal their indifference or opposition to God. Your desire to please God will show their desire to please themselves more clearly. Whatever you do and wherever you go, you will be a light that will reveal the deeds of darkness. You will also be like a lighthouse that shines through the night, leading ships to safe harbors. Rest assured that your life, once given wholly to God, will impact your workplace with the powerful truth of Jesus Christ. You will be surprised by the people who will notice your life and come to you inquiring of the difference between your life and that of others. They will see Christ shining through you.

YOUR CHURCH

The life God refines will also impact his church. Charles Sheldon's book *In His Steps* shows what God can do in a church when he has access to one life ready to be used. Charles Sheldon began to take seriously his commitment to Christ. He asked one simple question each time he had a decision to make, "What would Jesus do?" His life radically changed, and he began to affect others. A small group in his church began to follow his example, and his whole church was quickly transformed. Their commitment to follow the leadership of Christ impacted their entire community and city.

Once transformed by the refining power of the Holy Spirit, your life can't help but impact your church. God will lead you to ask the tough questions in business meetings and in committee meetings—questions like:

▸ What would Jesus do?
▸ Have we seriously sought the Lord's will in this matter?
▸ How can God use this to bring glory to himself?

You will begin to notice God's leading the church in particular directions of outreach and ministry. You will sense areas God is leading your church. And, just as in your workplace, you will begin to make others around you feel uncomfortable.

Your church may start to realize just how little they actually depend on God. In fact, your church may realize that if God were to remove his Spirit entirely from your church, there might be little change from the regular activities. A man who is being refined can help a church see its true state of holiness and separateness from the world (1 Pet. 2:9). God can use you as an instrument to bring revival and spiritual awakening to a people who are spiritually dry and thirsty and of little use to the Master.

God wants to use you in your present area of ministry such as a Bible study class or a children's program. Wherever the Master has placed you, you can act like leaven in bread (Matt. 13:33) or like a small mustard seed that grows into a large shrub (Matt. 13:31–2). God may also have such access to your heart that he can lead you to the ministry he has prepared for you.

THE ACTIVITY OF GOD IN OUR LIVES

The activity of God in our lives helps us to continue to be of use to God. Let's look at the implications of that statement through John 17:15–23.

JESUS INTERCEDES FOR US

Jesus could have remained on earth after his resurrection and continued his ministry in Galilee, but his plan was to work through those who believed in him to reach the world (John 17:9, 11). He sent the Holy Spirit as our comforter and guide (John 14:26). He continues to intercede on our behalf before the Father (Heb. 7:25) along with the Holy Spirit (Rom. 8:26–27). Christ knows the help we need from day to day: "We do not have a high priest who is unable to sympathize with our weaknesses, but we have one who has been tempted in every way, just as we are—yet was without sin" (Heb. 4:15).

GOD KEEPS US FROM THE EVIL ONE

God does not take us out of the world; rather, he keeps us from the evil one (John 17:15). We are Christ's hands, his feet, and his mouth while we are on earth (John 14:12). We are created in Christ Jesus to walk as he walked, to do the things he did while he was on earth.

None of us was an accident. Rather, we were each created by God to have fellowship with him and to be accessible vessels that God can use. The one challenge we face is given by the one who hates God most, Satan. He is the one who tempts us to do wrong. He is the one who schemes to destroy our relationship with God and render us useless to God. God alone has the power to rebuff Satan and render him powerless. Christ goes to God on our behalf to bind Satan's attempts to destroy us. He intercedes for us continually!

THE FATHER SANCTIFIES US

The Father sanctifies by truth (John 17:17, 19). Christ asked the Father to sanctify us by the truth and then said, "Your word is truth" (v. 17). Paul talks of Christ giving himself up for the church "to make her holy, cleansing her by the washing with water through the word, and to present her to himself as a radiant church, without stain or wrinkle or any other blemish, but holy and blameless" (Eph. 5:26–27). Sanctification is the process by which we are made holy. This begins at conversion when we are justified through Christ and lasts throughout our lives as the Holy Spirit continues his work. Sanctification is accomplished primarily through God's Word. As we encounter God in his Word, he reveals to us things about ourselves, about himself, and about others. We then are obligated to act on those revelations, or we live in disobedience. As we obey the revelations of God, we continue in the process of our sanctification.

> SANCTIFICATION—THE PROCESS BY
> WHICH WE ARE MADE HOLY.

Christ shows the importance of our sanctification in his prayer for us in John 15. We too ought to see it as a part of the refining process in being used by God.

JESUS SENDS US

Jesus sends us into the world (John 17:18). Second Corinthians 5:20 says, "We are therefore Christ's ambassadors, as though God were making his appeal through us." Christ has given us "the ministry of reconciliation" (2 Cor. 5:18), a ministry he began when he was on earth. When Christ said, "As you sent me into the world, so I have sent them into the world" (John 17:18), he meant that we were to have the same relationship with him as he had with his Father—the same trust, love, and dependency. "I am in my Father, and you are in me, and I am in you" (John 14:20). What a comfort to know we are not out on our own trying to make a difference in the world, but we have been chosen, appointed, and sent by the King of kings and the Lord of lords to be his ambassadors of light! We go on his authority, his power, his strength, on his terms, and with his protection. We are sent bearing a message of hope in a hopeless world.

CHRIST UNITES US

Christ intercedes for union with God (John 17:20–21). Unity is perhaps the single most important factor in the success of Christians. "'Every kingdom divided against itself will be ruined, and every city or household divided against itself will not stand'" (Matt. 12:25). Unity happens when "'two of you on earth agree about anything you ask for, it will be done for you by my Father in heaven. For where two or three come together in my name, there am I with them'" (Matt. 18:19–20). Christ is found in the midst of unity and agreement.

The spirit of division came into mankind in the garden of Eden with a deceitful serpent. Paul warned about those in our midst who cause divisions and put obstacles in our way (Rom. 16:17–18).

Division has caused the downfall of families, churches, denominations, and countries. No wonder Christ felt it important to pray to the Father for our oneness with him. Christ demonstrated perfect unity and oneness with his Father while he lived on earth. Through his unity with the Father, Christ was able to withstand temptations, false accusations, unending harassment, betrayal, and death.

We have the same Spirit as Christ. This Spirit brings us into perfect union with the Father as we are obedient, faithful, and yielding to God. Christ says that the purpose for our oneness with him and his Father is "to let the world know that you sent me and have loved them even as you have loved me" (John 17:23). God's single-minded purpose is to redeem a lost world. We have been redeemed, and now we are joining God in his mission to reclaim souls. Everything we become, through the power of Christ working in us, is for the purpose of reaching the lost around us. We are not being refined just to be holy but to be used by God to reach lost souls. We are not to reach unity simply to enjoy one another's presence in fellowship and worship but so the world may believe Christ was sent by the love of God to redeem them for eternity.

Jesus Gives Us His Glory

Christ gives us his glory (honor, praise, separateness) so we may be one—united together in heart and mind (John 17:22). This, indeed, is a great honor and one that should not be taken lightly. We have been prayed for by the Creator (John 1:3) to his

Father who gave us his glory, the glory that the Father had given him, so that we may be one as he and his Father are one. Since this is true, we have to work hard to bring division among our fellow Christians. We have to work against the prayers and the glory of Jesus Christ himself to bring deliberate strife or disunity into our relationships with others.

Christ's prayer found in John 17 is one of the most relevant prayers for Christians. It is a transparent, intimate look at Christ's relationship with his loving Father. When you pray, do you have a sense that you are speaking to your Father in heaven who loves you, who lives in you, and who guides you daily through all the enemy has sent your way? This prayer was said just minutes before Christ was unjustly arrested, tried, and then crucified for your sins. Does that add further meaning for you? Take time to read and reread John 17, keeping in mind it was the last recorded prayer of Christ for you before he suffered a torturous death on a Roman cross for your sins.

THINK ABOUT—PRAY ABOUT

After reading in the Bible about these men God used, do you understand that you are not different from them? God did not use men because of their skills; God used them because of their willingness.

▸ Think about your response to God. Are you trying to serve him based on your skills, or have you offered God yourself to use in any way he chooses?

▸ Have you ever had to ask God to forgive you? When you did, did you do so biblically? Did you pray, "Oh heavenly

Father, I come in desperation before you today pleading for forgiveness and a restored relationship with you, against whom I have sinned. And Father, please forgive me in exactly the same way I have forgiven those who have sinned against me"? Most men have said the Lord's Prayer a thousand times, but few take it seriously. We expect a lot from God, but we do not take seriously what he expects of us in a covenant relationship.

▸ Think about a time in your life when you encountered the discipline of God. Read Hebrews 12:10–11. Pray a prayer of commitment to obey God and receive his discipline as a sign of his love for you.

▸ We have tremendous potential to glorify God if we will obey him and accept his discipline in our lives. Pray for God's refining fire in your life as it affects your marriage, family, workplace, and church. Thank God for his love and discipline.

▸ Think about God's activity in your life as you reflect on the following passage. "God 'will give to each person according to what he has done.' To those who by persistence in doing good seek glory, honor and immortality, he will give eternal life. But for those who are self-seeking and who reject the truth and follow evil, there will be wrath and anger. There will be trouble and distress for every human being who does evil ... but glory, honor and peace for everyone who does good" (Rom. 2:6–10).

Chapter 4

THE GODLY MAN'S RESPONSE TO GOD

The Word became flesh and made his dwelling among us.
We have seen his glory, the glory of the One and Only,
who came from the Father, full of grace and truth.

—John 1:14

W hat makes a man godly? It isn't his good deeds or pleasing attitude. It isn't the sacrifices he might make for others or even the stands he takes. What makes a man godly is the presence and guidance of God in his life. All of us have been affected in some way by people we have met or experiences we have had. Consider the impact of having encountered a holy God through Christ. The result of God's presence in a man's life is a growing relationship with God that results in love for, and obedience to, God.

A man's relationship with God affects all of his relationships—with family, neighbors, coworkers, and even with his concern for people he does not know. A godly man's relationship with God will impact not only the present but, as the Bible often shows, the future.

As a godly man encounters God, he must seek to hear and recognize what God is saying to him. His hearing and obeying could have consequences for generations to come and be the key to others' sharing eternity with Christ.

IN DOING HIS WILL, WE EXPERIENCE GOD

My father was a machine gunner in the first World War. He fought at Vimy Ridge, where he was wounded and many thousands of lives were lost. He told me of one day when his commanding officer ordered him to take his men out of the trenches and across a field that had been mined by the enemy. He was to wait for the mine expert to lead him and his men safely through. When the expert arrived, he said, "I will take you across on one condition: whenever I tell you to do something, do it without question. It will mean your life and mine if you don't." The expert took my father and his men safely through the field. My father's future, as well as his children's and grandchildren's futures, depended on his obedience that day.

Our world is full of land mines planted by the enemy. Our loving heavenly Father knows just where they are planted and asks us to walk with him safely through them. Our future and the futures of our children depend entirely on our obedience to the expert. Jesus said in John 16:7, "It is for your good that I am going away. Unless I go away, the Counselor will not come to you; but if I go, I will send him to you." The Holy Spirit is our teacher, and he will apply God's Word to our hearts.

Reading Scripture is a personal encounter with God. God reveals himself to us through his Word by the Holy Spirit. Because this is an encounter with God, whatever you do next reveals what you believe about God, and it will determine whether you will truly experience God. You cannot experience God outside of doing his will. By following God, you will know and experience God's using your life.

When the disciples began to do what Jesus said, they saw how the multitudes were fed. When Moses obeyed God, the waters parted, and God's people were delivered from captivity. Throughout Scripture, men heard instructions from God and began to follow them; and in doing so, they experienced what God had said. Don't confuse understanding with doing. Some of us feel if we've read the Scripture and understand it that God's revelation is automatically going to happen. It won't automatically happen until we adjust our lives and begin to be obedient to what God has said.

Scripture is not a concept; Scripture is a person (John 1:1, 14). When you stand before the Word of God, you are not merely encountering a concept; you are standing face-to-face with God. Your response to him will be radically different from standing before a book. The moment you choose to read his Word, you choose to come into his presence, face-to-face. When you stand before God, whatever you do next reveals the nature of your relationship to him. You cannot go away from his presence and say, "I'm going to discuss this with my wife to see if we're going to obey or not" without offending him. The truth of God is not settled in a discussion.

The Word is a person. The Word is God speaking to you and me. The Word became flesh in Jesus Christ and lived among us.

The Bible is our opportunity to know Jesus better and for him to speak to us. The Holy Spirit will instruct and guide us in doing the will of God as we study the Word of God.

We've been coming to the Bible looking for points to discuss and issues to debate far too long. We must get back to what Christ said: "'The words I have spoken to you are spirit and they are life. Yet there are some of you who do not believe'" (John 6:63–64).

As Christ lived in the Father, so too must we live in him. "Man does not live on bread alone but on every word that comes from the mouth of the LORD" (Deut. 8:3). The Spirit uses the Scriptures to bring us face-to-face with God. The Scripture is his instrument through which the personal encounter can happen. When the Spirit of God reveals himself through the Scriptures, it is not a concept he is revealing to us but God himself.

John 3:16 is a familiar verse to many. But it is also a remarkable revelation about God. It reveals that God loved the whole world, not just some certain groups of people. It reveals that he loved those who knew him and those who did not. It reveals that his love extends to giving his own Son to die for us so that whoever believes in God's love will escape death and have everlasting life. From this familiar verse, we learn much about the love God has for us and the relationship of love he desires from us.

The person who loves Christ will do what God says. However, he will struggle with his obedience to Christ if he doesn't love God. If anyone tries to obey Christ without loving him, it will be a burden and a duty. He will never experience the joy and blessings that Christ intends for him to have. If a person has lost his first love, he will be a Christian who serves out of duty, loyalty to a church, obligation to others, or out of guilt from sin, but not out of love.

Jesus said, "'If anyone loves me, he will obey my teaching. My Father will love him, and we will come to him and make our home with him'" (John 14:23). You can participate in religious activity without a relationship with God. Many do. But if you are serving from these motives, you will miss experiencing God the way he created you to experience him. Everything in your life will be meaningless and fruitless. Your love for him determines your obedience, and your obedience determines your experiencing God. We love him because he first loved us (1 John 4:19). Don't lose heart in obeying God.

Love for God causes you to want to do what he says. It keeps your "doing" from becoming burdensome and causes you to find joy in your obedience (John 15:9—11).

The Bible says of Jesus, "Although he was a son, he learned obedience from what he suffered and, once made perfect, he became the source of eternal salvation for all who obey him" (Heb. 5:8—9). Jesus learned obedience through suffering. Men today are not willing to suffer and often avoid pain at all costs. If our marriages are in decline, we divorce. If our teenagers rebel, we throw them out of our homes. If we have pain, we search for a drug to end it. Pain is our body's alarm system. Pain tells us something needs immediate attention. Pain in the Christian life leads to a focused alertness to the activity of God, whose purpose is to lead us to obedience. If we felt no pain when we were disobeying God and, therefore, had nothing to restrain us, we could self-destruct.

Jesus Christ also learned obedience in his relationship with God. Jesus' daily communion with the Father was his source of strength and direction. "'My Father is always at his work to this very day, and I, too, am working.'... 'I tell you the truth, the Son can do nothing by himself; he can do only what he sees his Father doing, because whatever the Father does the Son also does. For the Father loves the Son and shows him all he does'" (John 5:17, 19–20).

GOD SETS THE AGENDA

Christians love to plan. Short-range goals, long-range plans, objectives, and targets are all a part of this obsession with planning. This was how Saul functioned before Christ intersected his life and renamed him Paul the apostle. He was zealous for reaching his goal of ridding the regions of followers of the Way. But once Paul had an encounter with Christ, his agenda changed. His fervor and zeal focused on growing the kingdom rather than planning its destruction.

I know men who go the distance to reach a goal and feel they have done God a great service. They are doing lots of "good things," but they are not being obedient to Christ. Goal setting is man-centered. We celebrate reaching goals rather than obeying God. Too often we have accomplished much in our own eyes but pathetically little in the eyes of God. We cannot grow God's kingdom; only he can do that.

Paul wrote that he considered everything a loss compared to the greatness of knowing Christ Jesus (Phil. 3:8–10). This is from a man who accomplished a great deal just by surviving to write his letter to the Philippians, not to mention the many churches he planted in the many cities where he took the gospel. Paul's missionary journeys were remarkable. But what Paul found great in his life was the miracle of being able to know and love Christ. His greatest desire was to know Christ and share in his sufferings, and like him, be resurrected from the dead.

Have you known of congregations setting goals like these?

- ▸ Everyone will know Christ and follow him.
- ▸ Everyone will experience and demonstrate the power of Christ's resurrection.
- ▸ Everyone will fellowship by sharing in Jesus' sufferings.
- ▸ Everyone will become like Christ and so attain the resurrection from the dead when he returns.

Do you think a church will grow if its members seek to achieve these goals? The church would burst through its walls! People who earnestly seek to be found in Christ, who demonstrate the power of Christ in their lives, and who aren't afraid to suffer as Christ did to be raised again to eternal joy will draw other people to Christ in droves. Goals are not bad as long as we let God set them. How do we do that?

God will reveal to us only what is important for the moment. He may share with us a vision for where we are headed, like Moses' going to the promised land. But the immediate future can radically shift without notice. God revealed to Moses that he was taking his people to a destination, but for every circumstance and surprise in between, Moses had to rely on God for the details.

GOD IS OUR RESOURCE

God is not predictable, but he is consistent. Man's ways are different from God's ways (Isa. 55:8–9). As Christians, we will not automatically make every decision correctly. We must seek the Lord at every turn.

I once heard a key denominational leader say, "Men, we have all the resources we need to win America to Christ. Our resources are people and finances." He went on to describe a program he was launching later that year.

That mind-set has two major flaws. First, we cannot win anybody; that's God's task. Second, our resources are not "us and our money." Our resource in kingdom work is God. If we celebrate that we can bring in the kingdom of God with our people and our finances, God will not stand for it. God will bring our efforts to an end in quick order. We are a covenant people who carry his name.

I know if I spoke to this denominational leader and confronted him with his mind-set he would say, "Of course, we all understand that God grows the kingdom. That is just understood!" But if we have to add God as a footnote when we speak of winning the world, then the center of our lives is out of focus. God is not a footnote we add to legitimize our plans and programs. The man God uses knows that God is the essence of redeeming a people to himself.

Several years ago I talked with a group of church leaders in a major metroplex and asked them how their churches were doing. They all indicated they were seeing some growth. I then asked them how their cities were doing. They all agreed that violent crime had risen, that murders were rapidly increasing, and that corruption between state leaders and financial institutions seemed out of control. I wondered how this was possible. This was an area with a high density of churches and one of the highest ratios of church attendees. How could these Christians make so little difference in the world around them? They were reaching their building project goals and their high attendance goals. They had met a lot of good goals. But had they been obedient to the Master? The man God uses would grieve over the condition of his nation because, although all the goals were reached, the gates of hell stood firm.

When revival broke out in Wales in 1904–1905, bars closed, jails were empty, and prostitution ceased. Cities were radically affected. When the people of God are touched by the power of God and are obedient to the Word of God, they can turn a world upside down! We're to be salt and light. If in the presence of light the city increases in darkness, what is to be said about the light? Either something is wrong with it, or it is hidden.

GOD INTERACTS THROUGH PRAYER AND HIS WORD

I recall a time in my life when I prayed to God requesting something of him but kept seeing something different happen. I became frustrated. I had always been told that if God didn't answer my prayer I needed to be persistent in my prayer and keep asking God until it was answered—or that I had sin in my life which was preventing his answering. But somehow this time seemed different.

I decided that the only way I could find out what God was doing was to let him tell me what he was doing through his Word. So I continued reading the Scriptures at a time when I was praying in one direction, receiving something else, and wondering why.

I was reading Mark 2:1—12 when God seemed to say to me, "Henry, I want you to notice something here." Some men were asking Christ to heal their friend. They even carried him to the roof and lowered him down on ropes to get him close to Jesus. Instead of immediately healing the sick man, Christ said, "Your sins are forgiven." They wanted healing, and Jesus offered forgiveness.

I began meditating on this passage, especially on Mark 2:9—11. God said to me, "Henry, these men were asking for one thing, but I had so much more to give them. They wanted a gift from me, and I wanted to make them my children so they could inherit everything, including healing." If God had healed the man without forgiving his sins, he would have lost out on so much more God had to offer. When I realized this, I immediately prayed, "Oh, Lord, if I ever make a request and you have something better in mind for me, please cancel my request!"

This is the crux of how often we ask for something good when asking for whatever God has to give us would bring us the best. Jesus not only provided for a physical problem, but he also provided for the spiritual one as well. We must direct our prayers so that they do not limit God by our limited understanding. I have found over and over that God usually wants far more for us than we ask. Just read Ephesians 3:20 and 1 Corinthians 2:9. We generally "underask" God in our prayers.

When my son Richard was just a boy, I bought him his first bicycle (a blue two-wheeler with many accessories), and I hid it in the garage. Then I had the task of convincing Richard that what he really wanted for Christmas was a blue bicycle. I had in mind a wonderful surprise for my son. All he had to do was ask. The bike was there waiting for him. This is how I understand

God's working in relationship with us. You know what my son asked for that Christmas? A blue two-wheeler.

In 1 Thessalonians 5:16–17, we are told, "Be joyful always; pray continually." Ephesians 6:18 carries this command, "Pray in the Spirit on all occasions with all kinds of prayers and requests. With this in mind, be alert and always keep on praying for all the saints." God wants us to pray without ceasing. Then we will be in full communion with him at all times, and we will be able to walk in the Spirit.

Our ultimate goal as Christians is to be one with Christ as he is one with his Father. This means to be of the same attitude, mindset, and desires as Christ.

Prayer is one of the means whereby God interacts with us. I recall coming before God in a particularly difficult crisis time in my ministry. As I poured out my heart to God, seeking his wisdom and guidance, a particular Scripture reference popped into my head. This verse was not one I had previously memorized or recently read. In fact, I had no earthly idea what it could say. When I flipped open my Bible to the passage, it was exactly the answer, almost word for word, that I was seeking. God used his Word to speak clearly to me during my prayer time with him.

Too often, when we come before God in prayer, we start rattling off our requests. But, if we stopped first and humbly asked him what he wanted to give us, and then prayed for those things, what might God do? Matthew 7:11 tells us that God's approach to giving is to give good gifts to those who ask him. The gifts are good because he knows what we need. Most parents are attentive and committed to their children. This Scripture says that, even though we are evil, we know how to give good gifts to our children. How much more will our Father in heaven give good gifts!

Remember the process of how God uses a man. God chooses a man, calls him, prepares, and uses him. This will be important to keep in mind as you pray. It helps explain God's response to our prayers. For example, if a single man were to pray to God for a wonderful, godly wife of noble character, yet his character demonstrated that he was nowhere near ready to be responsible for a godly wife, God would refuse him the request. God will match his blessings to our character. How tragic it would be for a man of small character and unstable faith to be given the responsibility of a committed Christian woman whom God has been fashioning for his purposes. Her effectiveness in service to her Lord could be forever compromised by her husband's lack of godliness.

Should you seek a position of importance and influence to serve the Lord and not receive it, God may be saying to you that your character is not yet ready to handle the blessing of fame or fortune. God may deliberately withhold certain blessings because it would feed your character flaws and give opportunity for Satan to tempt you to sin. As our character becomes more godly and as we become more trustworthy and faithful, God is able to answer more of our prayers. God can then give us our heart's desires (Ps. 21:2) because they will not lead us to sin, and our character will be able to handle the blessings. The man God uses trusts that God knows best and will not withhold anything good from his servant unless, (1) it is for his protection, (2) it is in his best interest, and (3) God has something better in mind.

The man God uses is first encountered by God. If God chooses to make his presence known, you must first recognize it is God and recognize what he is trying to say to you. Also, you must recognize that God has the unconditional right to your life. God doesn't say, "Please." He is Lord of your life if you are a Christian. God has the right to help himself to your life anytime he wants. The essence of becoming a Christian is releasing your life into the lordship of Jesus Christ unconditionally. Without that release, there is no possibility of being born again by the Spirit of God. The essence of sin is rebellion, or refusing to acknowledge that Christ has the right to be Lord.

Before you were born, God knew you. Before you were saved, God was shaping your life. He was molding everything about you. From the day he saved you, God has had greater access to do that work. The Christian life is a relationship with a person who has taken upon himself the responsibility of shaping and molding you until you are the person he wants you to be. As you walk in your relationship with God, he will begin to unfold everything he has accomplished in you and make it real, personal, and complete.

> MEN IN THE BIBLE WERE NOT BORN PROGRAMMED
> TO DO WHAT THEY DID FOR THE KINGDOM OF
> GOD. THEY CHOSE TO RESPOND TO GOD'S INVITA-
> TION. IN THE FOLLOWING SKETCHES, LOOK FOR
> HOW EACH MAN RESPONDED TO GOD.

Abraham was encountered by God, who made a covenant with him. God wanted (1) to make Abraham into a great nation, (2) to make his name great, and (3) to bless those who blessed him if Abraham would obey him. Abraham simply had to respond in obedience, and God would then set in Abraham's character everything needed to accomplish what God wanted to happen through his life. And Abraham did!

Isaiah was not driven to please God until he had a personal encounter with God during a crisis time (Isa. 6). He was brought into the presence of God in his vision and given a divine invitation of service. He responded "Here am I. Send me!" This simple response changed his life forever. From that day forward Isaiah became a mouthpiece that God used to influence kings and to encourage his people. Isaiah was faithful, trustworthy, and obedient.

Jeremiah was chosen from before conception to serve God (Jer. 1:5). God had elected Jeremiah to be his prophet. Jeremiah's prophecies of doom made him extremely unpopular with the leaders, both political and religious, and he found himself carried into exile in Egypt. He remained faithful to God despite enormous opposition and ridicule. His faithfulness was a testimony to both the faithfulness and the judgment of God. Sometimes God will give you an unpopular message to share with others, but the goal of the message is to bring people back into a loving relationship with him.

The call of the disciples seems fairly straightforward. Jesus said, "Follow me," and they did. Jesus had been living and performing miracles in the Galilee region for some time before he called his disciples (Luke 4). They had, no doubt, heard of him, and they may have sat near him as he spoke of the kingdom of God.

Jesus will not call us to any task without first establishing a relationship with us to develop trust and faith. At the same time, the disciples did not have full understanding of who Christ was, and their obedience was based on the little knowledge they did have. Christ will encounter each of us on a level we can understand and obey.

Paul had a dramatic encounter unlike anyone else in the Bible. He also was given an assignment unlike anyone else's. Christ was well aware of Paul's education and background as well as his dogged persistence to eradicate believers. Christ encountered Paul in a way Paul needed. The encounter had maximum impact and brought immediate repentance and redirection in Paul's life. In Paul's mind, he had been vigorously serving God all along. But his encounter with Christ brought the blinding truth of his misdirected zeal to light. Although he was physically blinded, Paul could truly see for the first time in his life. Paul now could boast in Christ instead of himself. He could devote his life to the Lord he had been persecuting. More than fourteen years later he was given the mission of taking the gospel to the Gentiles. God had a lot of preparation to do in Paul's life before he was ready to be used.

GOD TAKES THE INITIATIVE

A group of fifteen Fortune 500 CEOs met with me not long ago. As we talked together, they were touched by God and realized he had placed them in strategic positions to have a major impact on lives and communities. We looked at Isaiah 11:2–5 together. These verses from the Book of Isaiah list the resources of God available to any man for decision making. These men realized they have access to God as their resource in making moral and ethical decisions.

"The Spirit of the LORD will rest on him —
> the Spirit of wisdom and of understanding,
> the Spirit of counsel and of power,
> the Spirit of knowledge and of the fear of the
>> LORD —
and he will delight in the fear of the LORD.
He will not judge by what he sees with his eyes,
> or decide by what he hears with his ears;
but with righteousness he will judge the needy,
> with justice he will give decisions for the
>> poor of the earth.
He will strike the earth with the rod of his mouth;
> with the breath of his lips he will slay the wicked.
Righteousness will be his belt
> and faithfulnes the sash around his waist."

                      (Isa. 11:2–5)

These Fortune 500 executives realized that, as Christians, they cannot make decisions according to what they see with their eyes or hear with their ears. Rather, they have to depend on righteousness, justice, and faithfulness when they make decisions.

When the Spirit of God rests on a man in the midst of the impossible, God does a mighty work. The condition is that God's Spirit of power will rest on the one who is humble and contrite. If you bow before Christ as Lord, he will raise you up in his strength, wisdom, and power. God's Spirit will issue an invitation to you to participate with God in his activity. It may be through his Word, through your prayer time, through involvement with other Christians, or through the circumstances in which you find yourself.

God's encounter always brings a specific response. The challenge of having an experience with God is that it has to be translated into action. Christ did not come to earth simply so his disciples could have a deeper understanding of who God is. Christ came to give sight to the blind, to free captives, to restore people to wholeness, and to bring them eternal life. In eternity we can focus on knowing God more intimately, for we will need all of eternity.

What does God intend for believers to be on earth? "You are a chosen people, a royal priesthood, a holy nation, a people belonging to God, that you may declare the praises of him who called you out of darkness into his wonderful light" (1 Pet. 2:9).

This verse says that God intends us to be a chosen people, a royal priesthood, a holy nation, and a people belonging to God. For what purpose? That God's people may declare his praises as the one who called them out of darkness into his wonderful light.

How a Godly Man Responds to God

A godly man responds to God in several ways. We can know if we are making a godly response by laying our responses alongside Scripture.

Fear of God

The godly man will respond to an encounter with Almighty God with awe, reverence, respect, and fear. Perfect love (God) drives out all fear (1 John 4:18). Initially this seems contradictory. But to respond to God properly, we need a balance like that of a healthy relationship between a father and his children. A father who is all love is permissive. A father who is all discipline is cold and harsh. God is neither permissive nor cold and harsh. If we presume upon God's love, we are in danger of responding flippantly or with too much familiarity. Thus we compromise our obedience to him. If we hold to too much fear, we obey out of obligation and out of the fear of punishment. The balance is in having a healthy respect and awe for a God who would stoop to fellowship with his creation while at the same time understanding that he cared enough to have his Son die in our place.

God's love transforms us. God's love casts out fears and develops our faith. God's children must accept his love on his terms. If not, they may filter it through their earthly experiences and consequently fear and mistrust it.

SOVEREIGNTY OF GOD

"He is Lord!" is a popular phrase, but do we understand it? A godly man understands God's love, but he also understands God's sovereignty. A godly man would never assume that men could frustrate or prevent God's will in his life. Other people can have absolutely no effect on whether God can carry out his will. Only we can determine that outcome through our obedience.

Christ is Lord! He is Lord of all or not Lord at all. No person has more authority (Matt. 28:18), more power, or more control than Christ. No one. Jesus has complete control over the physical world, including the weather (Matt. 8:26). Can you imagine the physical power, even if we could produce it, required to stop a wave? And yet, our Lord stopped the motion of millions of tons of water with his words. Christ also has lordship over our physical bodies, healing all kinds of sickness with his touch (Luke 4:40). Christ's lordship extends to power over death, restoring life in an instant (Luke 7:15). When we say Christ is Lord, we must remember that Christ is Lord over all. His power is infinite, far exceeding anything we could even imagine.

TOTAL OBEDIENCE IN FAITH

A godly man makes no demands on God, nor does he argue with God. Arguing indicates either a lack of understanding of what God has said to us or our unwillingness to allow him control of our lives. We do not know the mind of God, nor do we comprehend the generational effects our obedience or lack of it will have. Only God knows. For us to try to place conditions on how we will allow God to use us is arrogant, proud, and rebellious. It indicates a heart problem. Only total obedience will accomplish in our lives what God has intended. Remember the result of King Saul's partial obedience (1 Sam. 15:22–23). His kingdom was taken from him, and David was anointed in his place.

ACCOUNTABILITY

The man God uses is well aware that the kingdom of God has a system of checks and balances. God holds us to the commitments we have made to him. God gave his Spirit as a deposit guaranteeing what was to come, namely our eternal salvation (Eph. 1:13–14).

God has also guaranteed that we will be judged, and for that reason, we determine to please him (2 Cor. 5:9–10). I have often thought that a terrible judgment God could impose would be to reveal what could have been. Too often we may choose something "good" instead of waiting for God to reveal his "best." The Bible tells us that we will reap what we sow (Gal. 6:7—8). Many consider this verse to remind us that we are accountable for our sins. But it is also a reminder that when we sow to "please the Spirit," God wants to guide us to the best harvest for his kingdom.

Whatever you do, work at it with all your heart, as working for the Lord, not for men, since you know that you will receive an inheritance from the Lord as a reward. It is the Lord Christ you are serving (Col. 3:23—24).

JOY

"'If you obey my commands, you will remain in my love, just as I have obeyed my Father's commands and remain in his love. I have told you this so that my joy may be in you and that your joy may be complete'" (John 15:10—11). Our natural reaction to an encounter with God will be joy. What a privilege, what an honor, what a miracle, that God would want to commune with me and count me worthy to act on his behalf in a world of need!

The man God uses will display a true picture of what the Holy Spirit's nature is in his response to God. Isaiah and Jeremiah provide two great descriptions of this:

> "My servants will sing
>   out of the joy of their hearts"
>
> (Isa. 65:14)

> "When your words came, I ate them;
>   they were my joy and my heart's delight,
> for I bear your name,
>   O LORD God Almighty."
>
> (Jer. 15:16)

HUMILITY

The man God uses will respond with deep humility, recognizing who he is in relation to God. We are the created; God is the Creator. For us to accept a divine interaction with pride or selfishness will cancel God's request of us. We ought never to consider that God has decided to use us because of our abilities or intellect. Pride will immediately compromise our effectiveness (Prov. 16:5).

ENCOURAGEMENT TO OTHERS

The man God uses is not critical but patient, forgiving, and gracious to others. He encourages those who need a word from the Lord. His faith will be a model for others.

I had the privilege of beginning a small Bible school in one of the congregations I pastored. I soon needed fellow pastors to come and teach with me as the number of students rapidly increased. I recall asking a pastor four hundred miles away to teach with me on a weekly basis and to trust the Lord to provide the finances to allow this to happen. I remember his words, "Henry, I don't see how in the world it's going to happen, but according to your faith, I believe it will be done." He was faithful, and his life was forever changed because he was. The response of the man God uses can profoundly impact others. His faith and obedience can bless those around him.

The Scriptures have many examples of how one man encouraged another. Jonathan was David's soul mate and saved his life several times (1 Sam. 20). Elijah the prophet was a mentor to Elisha, who learned from him, and God did twice the miracles through Elisha as his predecessor (2 Kings 2:9–25). Paul was a spiritual father to young Timothy and guided him into effective ministry (1 Tim. 1:2). Barnabas not only helped the new convert Paul to get grounded in the faith (Acts 11:25–26), but he also took on the timid John Mark, who would be the first to write a book on the life of Christ.

Investing in others' lives is no small thing. A Sunday school teacher asked a young boy named Billy to pray with him to accept Christ. Billy became Dr. Billy Graham, the noted evangelist used mightily of God around the world.

THE RESPONSE OF THE MAN GOD USES INVOLVES GOD'S PEOPLE

God's redemptive plan involves the whole community of believers. When we enter into his kingdom, we become a part of his chosen people, a royal priesthood, a holy nation, a people belonging to God (1 Pet. 2:9). We function within a body of believers, a church. The church is the body of Christ, with Christ as the head of the body. Each time he encounters us and reveals to us his will and intentions to us, it will have an impact on the entire body as we obey him. God's revelations to individuals are given in the context of the church, his body, a body that is equipped to carry out his will. As we share what God is saying to us, church members will pray for us, join with us, and hold us accountable to the calling God is giving us.

Part of our role as his servants is to use our God-given revelations to equip others for ministry (Eph. 4:12). Never think that you are a lone Christian. "Now to each one the manifestation of the Spirit is given for the common good" (1 Cor. 12:7). God will use fellow believers to confirm what he is telling you in his Word.

"In all things God works for the good of those who love him, who have been called according to his purpose" (Rom. 8:28). The church is the primary example of how God can put so many diverse and otherwise unrelated people together as equals to accomplish amazing feats.

GREATER USEFULNESS TO GOD AND MAN

A godly man's response makes him usable to God and effective in ministry to others. Each time the man God uses is obedient to his encounter with God, it prepares him for the next task. God often builds on previous tasks, increasing responsibility and importance.

As a teenager, my son, Tom, accepted God's invitation to lead a weekly youth Bible study in a small town fifty miles away. He planned the activities and study time and built relationships with the youth. Tom then served on a Christian student council while at the university, first as a committee member, and eventually as president. Meanwhile, he accepted the task of leading a choir at his church and served on the missions committee. He was faithful to all of the assignments God gave him. Soon God took Tom to Norway on a two-year mission program as a youth pastor where Tom used the skills he had learned serving on the student council and leading the youth Bible study. Eventually, Tom completed seminary and was able to serve a number of churches in combination positions as youth, music and education minister. He even has been able to serve his national convention as a consultant in both worship and discipleship. In each place of ministry, Tom sought to do the best job he could, never knowing where the next place of service would be. God found

Tom to be faithful in small things and began to give him more challenging tasks with greater responsibilities. The skills he developed in each place of service enabled him to serve in the next place of ministry God led him to.

God is able to see your life as a whole picture. God knows where he is taking you and what skills and abilities he will have to develop in your life for you to be effective down the road. View every task God gives you as critical. Try looking at your life from God's viewpoint. Consider how you currently serve God. How has God prepared you over time and used places of service to prepare you for other tasks? God will use your life.

EFFECT ON THE WORLD

If you take responsibility for your relationship with God, it will impact your marriage, children, neighbors, and others. When God makes a covenant with a man, it traditionally includes his descendants as well. Our faith is one of the most important aspects of our lives that we pass on to our children. Our relationship with God ought to permeate every relationship we have, especially with our children.

God sees it this way: "'As for me, this is my covenant with them,' says the LORD. 'My Spirit, who is on you, and my words that I have put in your mouth will not depart from your mouth, or from the mouths of your children, or from the mouths of their descendants from this time on and forever,' says the LORD" (Isa. 59:21). The presence of God in your life will impact the future.

When my children began to have their own children, I determined to take my responsibility as a grandfather seriously. At the birth of each of my grandchildren, I wrote them a letter. In the letter I mentioned a few things about the state of the world they came into and about the faithfulness of God to them as they were, indeed, answers to prayer. I also wrote that I would always be available to them if they ever needed me. When one of my grandsons turned six, I wrote another letter reaffirming my commitment to him and reminding him of my prayers for him. I received a note in the mail from him not long after that. In the letter was a cutout footprint with his name carefully printed in large letters on the front. As I turned it over, his mother had written for him on the back, "Grandma and Grandpa, I want you to know that I asked Jesus into my heart!" I was overjoyed. I regularly pray for my grandchildren, and one by one they are coming to know the God of their grandparents and their parents.

Even though your children may be out on their own, you still have a spiritual responsibility to them and their children. Grandparents can have tremendous influence on their families even if only through their prayer lives. For some reason, grandchildren see their grandparents as wiser than their own parents. This is a prime opportunity to tell them of God's faithfulness to you and his faithfulness to them.

If you haven't already, I hope you have made a deliberate plan to impact your children, grandchildren, and great-grandchildren with your faith. You may need God to bring healing to some relationships before your faith will influence them.

Start by reading Psalm 78:2–7. Then take a moment to review your family relationships, especially your relationship with your children. If they are more knowledgeable about your faults than your faith, you may need to ask their forgiveness before you can share your faith with them. Pray for the right things to say and do so "they would put their trust in God and would not forget his deeds but would keep his commands."

Our response to God will also affect our public life, where we work, and how we interact with people. Ernest Manning was born in 1908 and grew up on his father's homestead farm in Canada. He learned of God through his parents and came to know Christ as a teenager. He sought religious training at a Bible institute run by William Aberhart, a well-known radio evangelist. After graduation, Manning's passion turned to politics, and his compassion for the misery of people during the depression inspired his platform of social responsibility with political accountability. Manning replaced Aberhart after Aberhart's death in 1943.

Manning was first elected to public office in 1935 and elected premier of Alberta, Canada, in 1943. He governed his province for the next twenty-five years, winning seven consecutive elections, and retired in 1968 at the height of his power. His administration was free of corruption. "His moral standing, juxtaposed with his popularity, made him politically invincible, due in part, to his inheritance of Aberhart's religious torch." Manning had a rare combination of intelligence and honesty that deeply affected his son, Preston, who grew up to lead a national political party that reflected the passions of his father.[1]

Manning's two great passions were Christian ministry and serving the people of Alberta and Canada. He found that he could combine Christianity and social action and that his relationship with God gave him the direction and wisdom to do so effectively. Manning not only led his people to social, fiscal, and political responsibility, but through his weekly radio messages, he also led multitudes into the presence of God.

THINK ABOUT—PRAY ABOUT

We have considered the godly man's response to God. Review what we have covered and highlight an area you need to focus on in your relationship to God. Pray about it and commit to strengthening that part of your relationship.

▸ God will reveal through our relationship with him his plans and purposes for us. God didn't call us to be successful. God called us to be obedient. The success is his doing, not ours. Our role is to be his servants and let him accomplish what he will through us.

▸ Take a moment to evaluate your community, your neighborhood, or your marketplace. Is the darkness getting darker because churches and Christians are busy, or is the light getting brighter because churches and Christians are obedient?

▸ The essence of salvation is the release of our control to God's control. Does God have absolute, immediate access to your life today? Or would something dramatic have to happen to cause you to turn your attention to God? Pray and release control of your life to God.

▸ How do you respond to God? Just like the CEOs I met with, you are in a strategic position to impact lives around you. Pray to God and allow him to be your resource in influencing those around you.

---

1. Information about Ernest Manning is taken from Sheldon Alberts, Rick Mofina, and Bob Bergen, "Front Page," *Calgary Herald,* 21 Feb. 1996.

Chapter 5

MADE FOR TIMES OF CRISIS

"Now this is eternal life: that they may know you, the only true God, and Jesus Christ, whom you have sent."

—*John 17:3*

C risis is often mistaken to mean "tragedy" or "threat." A truer understanding is that *crisis* means "a turning point." For the believer, a crisis of belief is a point at which that person either trusts and obeys God or places his own wisdom or interests above God's. A crisis of belief equals a moment of decision.

In that respect, a crisis becomes an opportunity to serve God and see God work. Opportunities aside, crises are not without stress. At such times, the strength and value of belonging to a local church comes to bear. A local congregation is a family created to act in times of crises. Their support can make all the difference for the man God uses in times of crisis.

THE CRISIS OF BELIEF

Just before midnight the new pastor received a call to meet with two families in crisis. An adulterous affair had been discovered. Both parties, with their spouses, had come together to "resolve" the matter.

This was the pastor's first crisis in his new church. In fact, it was his first Sunday. He met and prayed with the people for several hours. Over the next few months, the new pastor sought to bring reconciliation and forgiveness into the situation but to no avail. The affair continued.

The church immediately began to minister to the two broken families. But despite valiant efforts to stop the ongoing affair, it continued. The church was eventually forced to remove from the membership the adulterous couple, who both held leadership positions in the congregation. The pastor would not compromise his convictions as a servant of God, and he was faithful to uphold before the congregation God's standards for marriage.

The new pastor had set the standard for his ministry with his new church by acting faithfully during their time of crisis. The church could see that they were getting a man after God's own heart to minister among them. Through his actions he had honored God and stayed true to his knowledge of Jesus Christ. The pastor's faithfulness and the actions taken by the church were an encouragement to many other churches who were facing similar situations.

Perhaps you are dealing with a crisis in your life now, or maybe one has just passed. It may well be that God is using you as his instrument to bring hope, peace, or truth into the situation. Be careful not to be so focused on the crisis that you are unable to see God in the midst of it. God may want to reveal something about himself to you in the midst of the crisis, so be watchful.

Some men wrongly assume that God saved them simply so they could go to heaven when they die. Salvation is knowing and experiencing God. The by-product of salvation is spending eternity with him. Some like to focus on the by-product instead of the purpose. God intersects our lives for us to come into an eternal relationship with him.

When God is about to do a great work, he looks for a man and sets out to intersect his life. You may recall that when Moses encountered God at Mount Horeb, God said, "'I have indeed seen the misery of my people. . . . I have come down to rescue them from the hand of the Egyptians. . . . So now, go. I am sending you to Pharaoh to bring my people the Israelites out of Egypt'" (Exod. 3:7–8, 10).

God had in mind to free his people from slavery. He had prepared Moses for this time. In fact, God had chosen Moses from birth to save him from the infanticide Pharaoh had decreed. Now there was a crisis in the lives of God's people, and God revealed his plans to Moses and commissioned him to be a vessel through which God could work. God knew he could trust Moses to be faithful and obedient. Despite Moses' initial reluctance, God used Moses to set his people free. God has used many others during crisis times. All have had lasting influence throughout many generations because of their faithfulness and obedience to God.

A great man of faith, Hudson Taylor, once said, "All God's giants have been weak men, who did great things for God because they reckoned on His being with them."[1] The man God uses does not see a crisis as a distraction. A crisis is an opportunity for God to create a highway over which he can impact a people.

God can also use a crisis to develop our character to make us more usable to him. Crises can be an opportunity for God to serve those in need through us. The crisis may appear negative, but crises are a normal part of life.

In the Bible, God always sent his prophets during times of crisis. They were often God's last line of defense to avert judgment. Jonah, Elijah, Isaiah, and John the Baptist are examples of God's prophets who came in times of crisis. In the midst of a crisis comes a moment of decision. I refer to it as a "crisis of belief." We must determine what to do and whose advice to follow. Will we go with our instincts, or will we seek the Lord?

Joshua was a man of integrity whom God could trust. He had come from Egyptian slavery through the exodus event, and then had to wander for forty years in the wilderness due to the sins of his people. He had seen numerous battles, felt the elation of victory and the devastation of defeat. After a lifetime of seeing God at work, he made a profound statement that men still have to grapple with. "If it seems evil to you to serve the LORD, choose for yourselves this day whom you will serve, whether the gods which your fathers served that were on the other side of the River, or the gods of the Amorites, in whose land you dwell. But as for me and my house, we will serve the LORD" (Josh. 24:15 NKJV).

GOD USED HIS PEOPLE DURING CRISES

The Bible was written for several purposes. One purpose was to provide examples of faithful men as well as unfaithful men. We are to follow the examples of those like Christ, Paul, the disciples, and the prophets. Even men who were ultimately faithful to God failed at times and received God's discipline in order to bring them back into a healthy relationship with him.

God has continued to use those he has raised up to serve his purposes. The following are some examples of men God used during crisis times in history.

GOD USED MARTIN LUTHER

Luther (1483–1546) began serving God as a Roman Catholic monk. He diligently sought God's favor through penitence and self-inflicted pain. Luther experienced deep depression because he was not ready for God to reveal himself and his purposes. But when Luther became immersed in the study of God's Word, God revealed himself and his ways.

God's people were not free to read the Bible in their language. At that time men and woman had to purchase forgiveness from religious leaders. These church leaders prevented God's people from having personal, meaningful interaction with God.

Through his Word, God revealed to Luther that "the just shall live by faith" (Rom. 1:17 KJV). This was a revolutionary concept. Luther realized he could be justified by faith alone rather than by his works.

Luther faced a crisis of belief. Could he trust this revelation from God's Word in the face of all he had been taught over the years? In his heart he knew he must be obedient to God.

On October 31, 1517, Martin Luther posted his ninety-five theses on the cathedral door in Wittenberg. Like a shaft of light, they pierced the darkness of ignorance and lifeless religion, revealing the freeing truth of God's Word. The Protestant Reformation was under way.

People no longer had to pay another human being for forgiveness or grace; they could go directly to God! They could experience the personal relationship God intended.

GOD USED JOHN WESLEY

The most prominent leader of the Evangelical movement was the son of a priest in the Church of England and later became a priest himself.

God had other plans for John Wesley (1703–91). God's people were gaining salvation through faith, but they were not being taught and discipled from God's Word. While on a trip to Georgia to propagate the gospel, God intersected John's life with Augustus Spangenberg, a Moravian Christian, who challenged John to know Jesus Christ personally. Three years later, Wesley experienced the salvation he had been seeking, and his relationship with Jesus Christ became preeminent.

Wesley later realized that it was not enough to see people saved; they had to be discipled. God led him to develop a "method" by which new converts could be taught to live a Christian life. He grouped believers for intimate fellowship and moral and spiritual growth under a mature Christian leader.

At Wesley's death in 1791, there were an estimated 71,668 Methodists in Great Britain. After his death, a denomination was formally established called the Wesleyan Methodist Church. Men were evangelizing the lost, but God used Wesley to fulfill the rest of the Great Commission, "'teaching them to obey everything I have commanded you'" (Matt. 28:20).

GOD USED HUDSON TAYLOR

In 1865, J. Hudson Taylor (1832—1905) came to understand that no one was reaching the unsaved in China. God led him to organize the China Inland Mission to reach the regions in China left untouched by other Christian organizations. By 1914, there were more than one thousand missionaries on its rolls. Taylor never directly solicited funds but relied on prayer for recruits, for money to pay salaries, and for running the sending organization. When offered sponsorship of his organization by a wealthy man, Taylor declined because he felt the organization would last longer than God intended. God gave Taylor a passion for the lost and a desire to go "to the ends of the earth" with Christ's name.

> "ALL GOD'S GIANTS HAVE BEEN WEAK MEN, WHO DID GREAT THINGS FOR GOD BECAUSE THEY RECKONED ON HIS BEING WITH THEM."
> —HUDSON TAYLOR

GOD USED JONATHAN EDWARDS

In 1734 and 1735, the Great Awakening broke out in Massachusetts, largely due to the preaching of Jonathan Edwards (1703—58). The son of a Congregational pastor, Edwards was looked upon throughout the English-speaking world as one of the greatest philosophers since the days of the apostle Paul and Augustine. Edwards demonstrated both a "keen, penetrating intellect" and a mystical temperament.[2]

At age sixteen, Edwards graduated from Yale with highest honors. One of his seventy personal resolutions, which he reviewed weekly, states, "Resolved, To be strictly and firmly faithful to my trust, that in Proverbs 20:6, 'A faithful man, who can find?' may not be partly fulfilled in me."[3] God used both Edwards's intellect and his devotion to impact lives around him.

The church in New England had become complacent and distracted from its role as salt and light in a world of darkness. God needed a man through whom he could bring back the fire of the Spirit. Through his fierce repudiation of sin, Edwards saw a wave of conviction spread over whole communities. His preaching was slow and methodical when he delivered his famous sermon, "Sinners in the Hands of an Angry God." God used him to bring thousands to saving faith in Christ, and revival broke out spontaneously throughout the eastern colonies.

GOD USED DAVID BRAINERD

Jonathan Edwards described David Brainerd (1718–47) as one prone to melancholy and depression, who did not "proportion his fatigues to his strength."[4] Brainerd endeavored to know God as intimately as anyone could. He spent hours in prayer and meditation.

God called Brainerd to serve as his mouthpiece to the native Indian people of Pennsylvania. Riding horseback through severe winter conditions and laboring long and hard took a toll on Brainerd's health. Nonetheless, he continued in his faithful service for God to the Indians. He died at age thirty in the care of Jonathan Edwards, who published Brainerd's diary as an example of faithful service and loyal dedication to God.

GOD USED WILLIAM CAREY

William Carey's efforts were instrumental in beginning the first missionary society in England in October 1792. Carey (1761–1834), a humble shoemaker, began to feel an urgency toward the lost around the world. At a meeting of Baptist churches, he asked why they were not sending missionaries to distant lands to convert the lost souls who had not heard the gospel. He was told by the moderator, "Young man, when God is pleased to reach the heathen, he will do it without your aid, or mine!"[5] Undeterred and driven by the Holy Spirit, Carey packed his belongings, boarded a ship, and sailed to learn new languages and share the gospel. His obedience to God three centuries ago helped launch the mission activities that take the gospel around the world today. He is remembered as the Father of Modern Missions.

These men were not biblical characters. They were not following after Christ through the regions of Galilee. They served the same God we serve and studied the same Scriptures we study. However, each of these men was of great character and was used mightily of God. Not one was perfect. Each had flaws. But each was faithful to his Master and obedient to his leadership. Their success was not in their accomplishments but in their obedience.

God is not finished using faithful men. He continues to write new chapters on men of faith used mightily by God. Your name and mine can be included with those in Hebrews 11 if we are faithful to our co-mission. Most of us would say, "If we are faithful to our mission," but it is God's mission to redeem a lost world. We have a co-mission, *co* meaning "together with, alongside, jointly or on the behalf of another." We work with God to act in times of crisis. Pray and commit to God that you will work with Christ and his Spirit as God's ambassadors to other people.

WE LIVE IN TIMES OF CRISIS

Christians in each generation are responsible for reaching their own generation. We can have no effect on preceding generations, but we can have an impact on our generation and an incredible impact on succeeding ones through our prayers, example, children, resources, and more. But it depends on how available to God we are today.

We've looked at some of those who have gone before us to make a difference in their generations. We've felt their influence upon us and their inspiration as we see what God accomplished through them.

Hebrews 12:1 follows what many call the "Hall of Faith" chapter in Hebrews 11, which lists more than a dozen individuals noted for their faith, and many others who demonstrated incredible faith in the midst of strife, mockings, battles, torture, and death. Many of these individuals were used by God during times of crisis. The Bible says, "All these people were still living by faith when they died" (Heb. 11:13). And yet they had been persecuted, believed that they were strangers on earth and longed for a better country, a heavenly city that the Lord has prepared for them (Heb.11:16). They are now powerful witnesses to us as we are the faithful ones God is using to reach our generation.

"Therefore, since we are surrounded by such a great cloud of witnesses, let us throw off everything that hinders and the sin that so easily entangles, and let us run with perseverance the race marked out for us" (Heb. 12:1).

Surely we are in crisis today. A commonly quoted statistic maintains that more than 50 percent of marriages in North America end in divorce. Such a figure implies that many children come from broken homes. Crowded jails, sexual exploitation of children, corruption, spousal abuse, racism, immorality, mismanagement in business, church closings, street violence, the drug culture—each gives evidence that the world is in crisis. This is before even mentioning the civil wars, ethnic cleansing, germ warfare, famine, and disease that are prevalent on the international level.

Every culture and country throughout history has had troubles. But I believe we are in the midst of unprecedented levels of crisis today. God has placed us in a unique time in history to impact a world in desperate need of a Savior. Let's examine some of these opportunities.

CRISIS IN THE FAMILY

Nowhere is crisis more evident today than in the family. If there is going to be healing in our country today, it must start in the family. For the home to stay intact, healthy, and God-centered, the man God uses must demonstrate integrity of character as a father and husband.

A family had a son who rebelled against his father and mother, even though theirs was a godly home and the parents feared the Lord. The boy failed the tenth grade, which was the beginning of several years of deep hurt, brokenness, and sorrow for the parents.

As they sought God's guidance and direction, this father and mother made a commitment to persevere with their son. Well-meaning Christian friends counseled them to show love by telling the son to abide by the rules of the house or leave. God told them: "I had rules in my house too. How many times did you break my rules and sin against me? I never kicked you out of my home. Every time you sinned, I forgave you when you asked me." God told them to love their son in exactly the same way he loved them.

The father would often go before the Lord saying he didn't deserve such pain and hurt; God would remind him of his own sins. The parents were not content to let the world tell them how to raise their son. They continued to seek the Lord, pray for their son, and act toward him as they felt Christ would.

That father learned how to love his son just as God loved him. The day finally came when the son finished high school. He went on to junior college, then to a university. Now he has finished seminary, married, and started a family of his own.

This son saw a dad who loved him as God would. When God gives you children, he has eternity in mind. God wants to work through you as a father to affect eternity through your children. What you do to train, educate, and model for your children will impact generations.

The promise of Malachi 4:6 is that God will turn the hearts of fathers and children toward each other. Before we begin to apply that verse to our human family relationships, we must each ask ourselves, "Is my heart turned toward my heavenly Father and his to me?" This Scripture is a plumb line to measure against our hearts and the way we relate to our own fathers and children.

Few fathers in the Bible demonstrated flawless character. Even Noah, one of the most respected fathers because all his children followed him when everyone thought he was crazy (Gen. 7:13), had a problem with alcohol (Gen. 9:21). Fathers who earnestly seek to be men of character will make an honest attempt to pass on their faith, not their flaws.

CRISIS IN THE COMMUNITY

Our world is morally bankrupt. In so many ways our day is not much different from the days of Noah. God saw that the inclination of men was toward evil, thinking of what they wanted and their advantage, all the time. "The LORD saw how great man's wickedness on the earth had become, and that every inclination of the thoughts of his heart was only evil all the time" (Gen. 6:5).

Contrary to what many say, man is neither naturally good nor inclined to act in the best interests of others. Without Christ, men will hide the truth and exchange it for a lie (Rom. 1:25). This is the world we live in. This is the arena where we work and serve God.

God has put his Spirit in our lives to guide and teach us. He did this to give us power and wisdom to serve him each day. God also did it to protect us from the onslaughts of our adversary. We will be called to represent God as his ambassadors to a people who no longer hold to absolute truths.

Robert had been a teen drug addict and knew the hard side of life. But God intersected his life and gave him hope and a purpose for life. Robert felt sure that he could not change the world, but he was equally sure he could make a difference.

Robert ran for a position on the local school board and was elected chairman. He didn't know all God had in mind, but several major moral issues began to emerge. Gay-rights activists swarmed the school board meetings and used the local media to pressure the inclusion of gay-education curriculum to combat homophobia and heterosexism.

Special-interest groups tried to force placement of ungodly books in school classrooms. Other organizations proposed condom machines in school bathrooms. Robert believed his city needed a man of conviction to stand up for truth instead of political correctness.

As he established his position and challenged the interest groups, Robert was publicly slandered and scolded. He was falsely accused of immorality, blamed for society's ills, and constantly heckled during meetings.

Robert was called by God for a time of moral crisis in his city when the moral education of its children was at stake. God had prepared Robert for this time, and he was faithful to stand firm during the crisis. His character shone through in the midst of massive opposition.

What we can see in the dark, the way we move when we cannot see where we are going, is different from what we can see in the light. When we have light, we can understand more and act accordingly. That can mean even taking risks or enduring hardships we could not see without the light. Doing the will of God requires that we not shrink from the contest of suffering. God does not promise that everyone will eventually come around to do the right thing, if we persevere. The Scripture does say that when we persevere, we do the will of God and will receive what he has promised (Heb. 10:32–33, 36, 39, 40).

CRISIS IN THE WORKPLACE

God has placed his people in strategic places where he wants to make a difference. Each man in his workplace is a powerhouse for God to accomplish his will.

You will never know why you are where you are in the workplace if you are not watching for God's activity. You must remain sensitive to the Spirit at all times. God may call you at a moment's notice to be an instrument in his hands that he can use. The ordinary person becomes extraordinary in these times.

Kim felt like he was the only Christian teacher on the elementary school staff. At his school, the disregard for Christianity was subtle. Opposition was politely presented as "not wanting to offend anyone," and in order to show "respect for all religious views." Kim felt like a small light in a vast darkness. How could he present the school Christmas musical in the given framework without compromising his faith and commitment to God? Kim chose the theme "Festival of Lights" that would celebrate the various ways different cultures celebrate light.

The feature song of the program was about the star that led the wise men to a Savior. The clear Christian message of the song sowed some seeds. A fellow teacher had noticed something different about Kim. As they talked later, Kim was able to share his faith. Kim was faithful to his Lord and refused to be intimidated to share his faith in an environment where it was considered one of many views. Kim couldn't have known that within six months his coworker would be killed in a car accident. God will use his people to impact the lives of their coworkers where he has placed them. "Now this is eternal life: that they may know you, the only true God, and Jesus Christ, whom you have sent" (John 17:3).

CRISIS IN OUR NATION

Most people do not make a connection between the state of affairs in our nation and the spiritual state of God's people. The Old Testament demonstrates over and over how the surrounding nations and even the land itself were blessed when God's people were in right relationship with him (2 Chron. 7:14).

One of the best remedies in times of national crisis is spiritual revival. God is looking for men who will be his humble servants, faithful and holy with Spirit-filled lives that he can use in times of crisis.

A crisis to one person may be to another a minor setback or a personal challenge. Without God we are in constant crisis. With God we have creative opportunities to minister to others and learn much about God's character. The key is found in 2 Chronicles 7:14, humbly seeking God through prayer and repentance. This is the one God will use to "heal the land" of its pain and despair. Revival is for those who have once experienced life but are lifeless or wasting away. Revival is for God's people. Non-Christians need to have a spiritual birth. They cannot be renewed or revived until they come from spiritual death to life for the first time.

CHURCHES FOR CRISIS TIMES

As a Christian, you have been placed in a body of believers, interconnected and interdependent through the Holy Spirit. When one member hurts, the whole body hurts. If one member rejoices, the whole body rejoices (1 Cor. 12:26). It is not "my family's crisis" or a "personal crisis." A crisis should be seen in the context of happening in the church family; it is a corporate crisis.

This is what it means to be the body of Christ. Each member, with different gifts and abilities, is strategically placed in the body to serve others in times of crisis and in times of rejoicing. If you prevent the church from sharing in your personal crisis, you rob the church of doing one of the things it was designed to do.

A man I know enjoyed testing his church family to see how much they cared for him. Once he went to the hospital without telling anyone and then waited for people to visit him. No one came. He became indignant and angry with his church for not caring for him and eventually left the church. You can allow the church to minister to you in times of crisis, or you can prevent it out of pride or stubbornness.

Churches are the "world mission strategy headquarters" that God uses for his purposes. Churches are the sending agencies God uses to address the needs people have in times of crisis. Churches are to be constantly on mission with Christ redeeming a lost world. Jesus said, "'I will build my church, and the gates of Hades will not overcome it'" (Matt. 16:18). "'But I, when I am lifted up from the earth, will draw all men to myself'" (John 12:32). Christ desires to build his church and draw men to himself. That is his role. "The one who calls you is faithful and he will do it" (1 Thess. 5:24). Our role as a church is to be his body that he will use to accomplish his work through ministry to others.

A Sunday school teacher found out that one of his class members was in crisis. The member's wife was scheduled for carpal-tunnel surgery and would not be able to use her hand for some weeks. The couple had two children, and his job involved a great deal of travel. The teacher asked if he or the class could do anything to help. They appreciated the thought but did not seem to think much could be done. The teacher contacted class members to see how they would like to help. Before long, every dinner for two weeks was provided. The class was more than happy to help this family in crisis. The class member and his wife were not only surprised by the generosity of the class but were also overwhelmed that people would take the time to care for them and their family.

A young couple, who were living together, began attending church. He was an alcoholic, and their relationship was in jeopardy. The church began to pray for them, love them, and watch as God surrounded them with those who could help him deal with his addiction. Soon they asked how to accept Christ, be baptized, join the church, and be married! Even though they had no family, no money, and knew only a few people in the church, the wise pastor told them not to worry and to set a date for their wedding.

The pastor shared their needs with the congregation who understood the importance of being the body of Christ. The wedding took place at the close of Sunday morning worship. When the pianist started the wedding march, out came the groom with a church member at his side. Down the aisle came the maid of honor, another church member, followed by the bride. An older deacon escorted her down the aisle. After the wedding, the church provided a dinner in a hall that church members decorated. More than 150 guests attended, all members of their new family.

I can't begin to tell you how important the church has been to our family. When my wife almost died a few months after giving birth to our fifth child, the church was there to minister to us.

When I had to be gone often on Sunday afternoons to help start a mission church ninety miles away, the church family cared for our children. My father died just after the birth of my first son, and my mother died after my third son was born, so my children never knew their Blackaby grandparents. But they knew the senior adults of our church, especially three widows who slipped my children pieces of candy or small gifts and often asked how they were doing. More importantly, they regularly prayed for my children.

Nothing is more dear to a pastor than to have his church family minister to his children in a time of crisis. It is sad when a pastor feels he has to protect his family from the church. I found often that it was the church who protected my family.

If you are interested in growing as a Christian and coming to know what it means to be a part of the family of God, help your church know how they can minister to you in times of crisis. If you find that your church is not the kind of church we are talking about, don't leave; rather, help your church become the church God wants it to be!

I was meeting with a small group of Laotian Christian immigrants for Bible study in their house church. We talked about being salt and light. They told me that in their home country they soaked the bamboo in salt. After the salt had penetrated the bamboo, it was then possible to mold and shape it. They boldly exclaimed to me that as Christians they intended to be the salt that made it possible to shape the direction of their new country.

As the church goes, so goes the world. If salt loses its saltiness, it can't be used as a preservative. There is nothing to deter rotting (Matt. 5:13). Our world is in desperate need of those who can stand in the gap and prevent its destruction. If we are not preventing the deterioration of the world, the problem is not with the world; it is with us. We can't blame the darkness for acting like darkness; that's what it naturally does. But in the presence of true light, darkness has trouble maintaining its presence.

SETTING OUR PRIORITIES BY GOD'S AGENDA

Christ always had in mind the will of the Father. He had a mere three and one- half years to accomplish more than anyone had in the history of the world. In this short time Christ managed to fulfill a myriad of prophecies, effectively train a handful of disciples to continue his work, defeat all the powers of darkness and death, and become the one acceptable atoning sacrifice for the sins of mankind.

Jesus optimized the use of his time. Through his relationship with God the Father, Jesus was able to find the daily guidance for ministry he needed to fulfill completely all that God intended.

> "OUR LORD'S FIRST OBEDIENCE WAS TO THE WILL
> OF HIS FATHER; NOT TO THE NEEDS OF MEN; THE
> SAVING OF MEN WAS THE NATURAL OUTCOME OF
> HIS OBEDIENCE TO THE FATHER."[6]
> —OSWALD CHAMBERS

As Christians, we spend time with God each day so he will have opportunity to set his agenda on our hearts. This way nothing will be able to take us by surprise because the Father, who loves us, will have prepared us. God intends for us to access his strength, wisdom, and power to deal with what is coming our way, even as Jesus did. "'I pray for them. I am not praying for the world, but for those you have given me, for they are yours'" (John

17:9). But everything depends on our willingness to seek, love, and obey him.

A famous evangelist one day received a phone call from the president. When informed of the call, he continued his prayer time some fifteen minutes longer, putting the president on hold. Not being accustomed to waiting, the president asked what was so important that he had to wait so long. The evangelist replied that as soon as he heard he had a call from the president he knew the matter must be urgent. He had to seek the mind of God first in order to be of any assistance to his nation's leader.

One of the final assignments God has reserved for Christ is to return to earth to claim his loyal followers and to usher them into heaven, a place prepared for his saints. This will be a glorious event (John 14:2–3).

Christ promised also to return. This was certainly the one hope that caused believers under severe persecution to be faithful to the end (1 Pet. 4:17–19; 5:8–11; Rev. 2:3, 10, 13). Whatever persecution, slander, discrimination, or hurt the world may bring upon those who call on the name of the Lord will be worth the prize we all seek. Just like the apostle Paul, Christians around the world and throughout the ages have clung tightly to their belief that the one who was dead and is alive forever and ever will bring all of his faithful with him into his kingdom for eternity (1 Cor. 9:24–27).

INTENSITY FELT

While we wait for Christ's return, we have much to do. Time is short. No one in the New Testament demonstrated this better than Paul. Paul lived with the intense desire to bring as many people into the kingdom as he possibly could. Read what he said to the Christians in Corinth.

> "TO THE JEWS I BECAME LIKE A JEW, TO WIN THE JEWS. TO THOSE UNDER THE LAW I BECAME LIKE ONE UNDER THE LAW (THOUGH I MYSELF AM NOT UNDER THE LAW), SO AS TO WIN THOSE NOT HAVING THE LAW. TO THE WEAK I BECAME WEAK, TO WIN THE WEAK. I HAVE BECOME ALL THINGS TO ALL MEN SO THAT BY ALL POSSIBLE MEANS I MIGHT SAVE SOME. I DO ALL THIS FOR THE SAKE OF THE GOSPEL, THAT I MAY SHARE IN ITS BLESSINGS."
> (1 CORINTHIANS 9:20–23)

Paul ran the race in order to win. He modeled for every Christian a fervor and dedication to his God-given mission, like an Olympic contender of today. Paul wasn't one to settle for second place. Tradition has it that Paul was "faithful, even to the point of death," and that God had waiting for him the "crown of life" (Rev. 2:10).

URGENCY EXPERIENCED

Jesus tells several parables concerning his unexpected return (Matt. 25:1–13; 24:45–51). In one parable Jesus tells about two servants who were put in charge of their masters' households. One servant was found faithful to his responsibilities. When his master returned unexpectedly, he was rewarded accordingly. The other was wicked. He beat his fellow servants and ate and drank with drunkards. When his master returned and found him abusive and neglectful, he was assigned to "'a place with the hypocrites, where there will be weeping and gnashing of teeth'" (Matt. 24:45–51). We would be wise to "be about our Father's business" if we expect to be found faithful at Christ's return.

We cannot know when Christ will return. Just as we do not know when he may call us home to be with him, no one can know when Christ will return. "'No one knows about that day or hour, not even the angels in heaven, nor the Son, but only the Father.... Therefore keep watch, because you do not know on what day your Lord will come.... So you also must be ready, because the Son of Man will come at an hour when you do not expect him'" (Matt. 24:36, 42, 44).

The man God uses knows that there is only enough time allotted to each of us to complete the tasks God has prepared in advance for us to do. If we spend that time on our own desires rather than God's, the time we use is unrecoverable. "'For the Son of Man is going to come in his Father's glory with his angels, and then he will reward each person according to what he has done'" (Matt. 16:27).

ACCOUNTABILITY ACCEPTED

One of Christ's parables, the parable of the talents, spoke to the issue of accountability (Matt. 25:14–30). This parable speaks in clear terms about what God expects of his people. Each person has been given an opportunity for service that God intends to be used in his kingdom. A time will come when we will stand before the judgment seat of Christ and be held accountable for how we used what we were given, whether talents, gifts, resources, time, words, or actions—both what we do and what we neglect to do. Those who are faithful followers will receive heavenly rewards in accordance with their faithfulness. But those who are negligent, foolish, and untrustworthy will receive punishment and separation from God.

Christ also taught that one criterion for judgment is how closely we functioned within his will and in relation to him as Lord. It is not enough to go around doing good deeds. We must be obedient to the Master and accomplish what he has for us to do in relationship with him.

Based on 2 Corinthians 5:9—10, we should live our lives in preparation for judgment. "So we make it our goal to please him, whether we are at home in the body or away from it. For we must all appear before the judgment seat of Christ, that each one may receive what is due him for the things done while in the body, whether good or bad" (2 Cor. 5:9—10).

PRIORITIES DEFINED

Because our time is short on earth, it is wise to have our priorities as Christians in line with Christ. The Bible is full of guidelines for setting our priorities. Here are just a few that you can measure your own actions against.

"'Seek first his kingdom and his righteousness, and all these things will be given to you as well'" (Matt. 6:33).

"'Enter through the narrow gate. For wide is the gate and broad is the road that leads to destruction, and many enter through it. But small is the gate and narrow the road that leads to life, and only a few find it'" (Matt. 7:13—14).

"'Not everyone who says to me, "Lord, Lord," will enter the kingdom of heaven, but only he who does the will of my Father who is in heaven'" (Matt. 7:21).

"We are God's workmanship, created in Christ Jesus to do good works, which God prepared in advance for us to do" (Eph. 2:10).

"'If you love me, you will obey what I command'" (John 14:15).

The crisis of the lack of time will cause the man God uses to be heaven-minded while on earth. The old phrase, "He's so heavenly minded that he's no earthly good," can be rather misleading. In order for the man of God to be of any practical and meaningful use on earth, he must have the mind of Christ!

You can't be a pastor for long before you have someone sitting in your office weeping over the lost years spent seeking the things of this world instead of seeking first the kingdom. I remember speaking at the funeral of my godly mother-in-law, Carrie Wells. She raised three children: two missionaries and one pastor. Most of her grandchildren were there. Several had completed seminary and were in the ministry. Her eulogy was given by my eldest son who spoke of her devotion to the Lord and her faithful prayers for her children, grandchildren, and great-grandchildren. He described the impact she had on his life and how she modeled for him a true servant of the Lord. I recall watching as six grandsons lovingly carried her casket to the waiting hearse.

There were a lot of tears that day, tears of sorrow and tears of joy. Many of us rejoiced that she was finally freed from a deteriorating mind and body. But others were pierced to the heart that day because they realized that their funerals would be quite different. They had not lived lives pleasing to the Lord. Some were estranged from their children. They rarely saw, much less prayed for, their grandchildren. They spent life selfishly on things that would pass away, or they had a sense of grief over how little they knew about the one who would judge them and how little they had invested in representing Christ in relationships.

My mother-in-law had many friends. As I looked out across a sea of white-haired people in the service that day, I wondered how many years had been spent on eternal things. We never know how much time God is allotting to each of us. We should be spending it wisely.

You may think that with only three-and-one-half years for public ministry, Christ would have been frantically trying to go as many places as possible, to preach to as many people as possible, and to do as many miracles as possible. Instead, we see him slipping off to solitary places spending time in prayer. We read of his taking only a few men with him to witness his transfiguration on the mountaintop. Christ spent time talking with one woman here, a blind man there, a rich man late at night by himself.

The key was not the amount of activity Christ accomplished. The key was that he accomplished the right activities in obedience to his Father's will. The Son of God performed miracles and amazed the masses with his teaching. But above all else he was totally obedient to God.

Jesus demonstrated that the man God uses is not directed by situations or people. Jesus' followers thought they knew what would be best for him, such as when the disciples tried to stop children from being brought to him for blessing (Matt. 19:13–15). Jesus showed us that a crisis never forced him to act in haste or on his own strength, such as when he was summoned to come to his dying friend Lazarus (John 11:1–12:19).

Christ always took the time to seek the Father and act according to the Father's will in every situation.

THINK ABOUT—PRAY ABOUT

As you relate to God in your next prayer time, ask him to show you clearly where to invest your time and talents so they will bring back the return he wants. Consider where you are spending most of your time. Is it where God has placed you, or is it according to plans made apart from his leadership?

▶ God will lead you into situations that require you to make a decision. This crisis of belief is a fork in the road where you decide whether you will follow God. How you respond when you reach this point will determine whether God will be able to use you or whether you will go your own way and miss all God has purposed for your life.

▶ The man God uses will "live by faith, not by sight" (2 Cor. 5:7) when he encounters a crisis of belief. This will be a personal time for you. The ramifications of your decision will affect every relationship you have. Pray that your response to your next crisis of belief will honor God.

▶ God desires that we turn our attention from our circumstances to him. When our eyes are on him, our crisis seems so small. We, the created, stand before God, the Creator, who can do all things whatsoever he desires. Be sensitive to God's activity in your family, community, workplace, and nation. Spend time in prayer focusing on God's activity in each of those areas.

▶ Christ did not pray for the world but for his followers and for those who would believe because of them (John 17:9). Christ knew that they would be the key to saving a lost world. Pray that you and the men in your church will grow closer to Christ and live for him.

---

1. Hudson Taylor, as quoted by Warren W. Wiersbe, *Victorious Christians You Should Know* (Grand Rapids: Baker Book House, 1984), 14–15.

2. Kenneth Scott Latourette, *A History of Christianity* (New York: Harper & Row, Publishers, 1975), 959.

3. Jonathan Edwards, *The Life and Diary of David Brainerd* (Grand Rapids: Baker Book House, 1949), 20.

4. Ibid., 50.

5. J. I. Packer, *Evangelism and the Sovereignty of God* (Downers Grove, Ill.: InterVarsity Press, 1961), 33.

6. Oswald Chambers, as quoted by Wiersbe, 59.

BEING A KINGDOM CITIZEN

"For my thoughts are not your thoughts,
neither are your ways my ways,"
declares the LORD.
"As the heavens are higher than the earth,
so are my ways higher than your ways
and my thoughts than your thoughts."

—*Isaiah 55:8–9*

I saiah 55:8–9 reminds us that God's ways are not the same as the ways of the world. We know that what people have done through history, and what they might do today or tomorrow, usually does not reflect God's perspective. Their actions are examples of the ways of the world. The world does not rely on God. The world assumes that human goals are the highest good. The world's concept of the highest good is influenced and limited to the wants, desires, and needs of different groups of people.

God's ways demonstrate the power of God at work in every situation. From God's perspective, the truth of Jesus Christ is the filter for everything presented as truth. God's ways provide his people all that is available from God—his wisdom, power, grace, patience, and provision. A person who functions according to God's ways is more than a resident of this world; he has become a kingdom citizen functioning according to kingdom ways.

GOD'S WAYS ARE NOT MAN'S WAYS

One of the most absurd military tactics ever recorded was in Joshua 6:1—27. Once a day for six days, Joshua marched Israel's soldiers and seven trumpet-playing priests around the walled city of Jericho carrying the ark of the covenant! They marched and played trumpets.

On the seventh day their instructions were different. Joshua and the soldiers marched around the city seven times instead of once. When they heard a long blast from the trumpets, they were to shout at the walls. Not attack them, besiege them, or build a rampart—just shout at them.

This plan would have been ridiculous had it come from Joshua. But it came from God, and no one questioned it. God didn't need anyone to march around the city to bring the walls down. In fact, God didn't even need the walls to come down to destroy the city. What God required was a people ready to do whatever he commanded. For the Israelites, obedience meant the difference between life and death. God had something to teach his people about himself, and he used Joshua's faithfulness to bring it about.

When God revealed his power and faithfulness to his people, all the kings in the surrounding region were afraid. Never before had they encountered the might of God. But God was far more concerned about revealing himself to his people than about knocking down city walls. Obedience was the key, even when it didn't seem to make sense. God's ways are different from our ways, and his kingdom is different from the kingdoms of this world.

MAN'S PERSPECTIVE
IS DIFFERENT FROM GOD'S PERSPECTIVE

We think finances. Jesus says eternity. We think busy schedules. Jesus says eternity. We think a new car. Jesus says eternity. We think lose weight. Jesus says eternity. We think burnout. Jesus says eternity. We think comfort. Jesus says eternity.

To think in terms of eternity, we need to have the mind of Christ. God's Word tells us that God's people should be different from the world (Rom. 12:2). In fact, in the wake of a transformed life and renewed mind, we could expect to differ from the world by how we test and approve God's will. This cannot but make a difference when, from God's perspective, we look at our ministry involvement, business decisions, where we work, our marriages, interaction with our children, health problems, or losing a loved one. Focusing on God's ways in these areas will transform our lives.

God created us not for time but for eternity. He always works from eternity to eternity. God will work in the midst of time, but he always has eternity in mind. If you make decisions in your life based on time, you will make them one way. If you make the same decisions based on eternity, you will come to a different conclusion. When God works in your life, he'll bring you to a broader dimension in his kingdom.

You may have had an experience when you encountered God with an unusual intensity. It may have been in a small-group meeting or a large rally held in a stadium. It may have been at a Bible study or prayer time. It may have been during a quiet time or a worship service. It may have been on a mission trip. But nothing seems quite the same now. You may feel restless. Perhaps you sense God has something much larger in store than you expected! You may even feel nervous, anticipating a deep life change. You just know God wants greater involvement with him for your life.

> "IT IS ALWAYS HELPFUL TO US TO FIX OUR ATTENTION ON THE GODWARD ASPECT OF CHRISTIAN WORK; TO REALIZE THAT THE WORK OF GOD DOES NOT MEAN SO MUCH MAN'S WORK FOR GOD, AS GOD'S OWN WORK THROUGH MAN."
> —HUDSON TAYLOR

This sense of something much larger may even involve your spouse and your family. It is important that you are clear on what God may be saying to you at this point in your life. You may be on the verge of experiencing God as never before, and there is a real possibility that your life may never be the same again!

KINGDOM WAYS

The kingdom of God is nothing like the kingdom of the world. This was one of the central truths Jesus systematically instilled into the minds of his disciples. It functions on different principles with different purposes. The kingdom is ruled by love, not power, greed, or ambition.

Jesus called a few men to follow him and then spent three and one half years teaching and training them about the ways of God's kingdom. They entered the kingdom of God (John 3:3—8) when they responded to Jesus as Lord in their lives. From that moment on, their lives would be forever changed. They would learn to see their lives from God's perspective.

Jesus often told parables to illustrate kingdom ways and how God's ways accomplish his work. Two parables are about the mustard seed and yeast, or leaven. Found in Matthew 13:31—33, these parables describe the kingdom way of starting things. "He told them another parable: 'The kingdom of heaven is like a mustard seed, which a man took and planted in his field. Though it is the smallest of all your seeds, yet when it grows, it is the largest of garden plants and becomes a tree, so that the birds of the air come and perch in its branches.'"

"He told them still another parable: 'The kingdom of heaven is like yeast that a woman took and mixed into a large amount of flour until it worked all through the dough.'"

The world seeks to make big impressions with immediate results. God starts small. If God has the essence right, he will cause growth, small at first, unseen and unobserved (like yeast in bread). But in the end his rule will be extensive and thorough.

One man submitted to God can impact a whole company or an entire community. A single student can impact an entire campus. One inmate can radically change a whole prison. One child can influence his whole family. One humble and obedient life can change an entire church.

Don't be discouraged if when you obey a command of your Lord you don't see immediate results or success. Don't leave or abandon a men's prayer group, Bible class, or prison ministry because results are not immediately visible and successful. If your life remains obedient to what your Lord has asked, he will ensure that what he purposed will come to pass.

This may be difficult for you to grasp because we have been trained to see things from the world's perspective. Let your life function from God's perspective. God wants the world to see and know him and his ways, not see you and the world's ways. Let God manifest himself through your life.

The missionary, Hudson Taylor, said, "It is always helpful to us to fix our attention on the Godward aspect of Christian work; to realize that the work of God does not mean so much man's work for God, as God's own work through man."[1]

Our lives take on new meaning and eternal purpose when we see them as being used for God's work through us instead of our work for God.

While the parable of the sower appears in Matthew 13, Mark 4, and Luke 8, the message is the same: God's Word is powerful and full of life, just like a seed, capable of multiplying many times where it is planted! When God speaks, and Scripture confirms it is the voice of God, you can count on God to accomplish everything he says. The key is the truth planted in the soil.

The soil is your heart and the hearts of those God is seeking to influence or affect with truth. This is true in your workplace, neighborhood, and home.

When you read and apply Scripture, you can be confident in the one who is present in the Scripture. God himself is always present, using his Word to affect the hearts and lives of people he loves and for whom Christ died. Trust what Jesus said in the parable of the sower to guide your witness and to give you confidence where God has placed you. The same kingdom principles Christ taught his disciples are at work in and available to your life today.

> ONE MAN SUBMITTED TO GOD CAN IMPACT A
> WHOLE COMPANY OR AN ENTIRE COMMUNITY.

The parable of the farmer and the seed is a favorite text for sermons, so it may seem familiar. However, it takes on fresh meaning when pondered again. For instance, read the parable and then ask yourself what would have happened if the sower had considered the path, the rocky places, and the thorns, then decided not to sow the seed at all.

"'A farmer went out to sow his seed. As he was scattering the seed, some fell along the path, and the birds came and ate it up. Some fell on rocky places, where it did not have much soil. It sprang up quickly, because the soil was shallow. But when the sun came up, the plants were scorched, and they withered because they had no root. Other seed fell among thorns, which grew up and choked the plants. Still other seed fell on good soil, where it produced a crop—a hundred, sixty or thirty times what was sown. He who has ears, let him hear'" (Matt. 13:3–9).

Many men have lived according to what Jesus taught his disciples, and they have seen God change lives, just as he said he would. A modern example is the ordinary men on mission trips who have obediently shared their faith and have seen others respond in saving faith to Christ.

Some men in the business community were moved of God to begin a Bible study. They obeyed God and trusted he was already working in their marketplace. They believed their business community was just like Jesus' parables on the kingdom said it would be. To their joy, others responded. Some, over time, were saved. Others found their marriages were changed. Still others returned to faithfulness to God through Bible study. God's Word was multiplied many times over in its effects on the lives in which it was sown. The truth changed lives.

Christian men must be kingdom citizens and function by kingdom ways. Jesus guided ordinary men such as fishermen, tax collectors, and students to live by God's ways. As his servants in their world, God worked through them to turn the Roman Empire upside down. Multitudes entered the kingdom because of their faithful witness. God has always done this. This is his way, and he can do it through your life too.

THE PARADOX

Christ often used ordinary situations to teach spiritual truth. Often his parables contain paradoxes—statements that seem to contradict themselves. For example, Jesus said if you want to save your life you must lose it (Mark 8:35); to be the ruler of all you must be the servant of all (Matt. 20:27); and to live you must die (John 11:25).

Spiritual truths often contradict what we accept as reality. Christ demonstrated lordship by washing his disciples' feet. In the world today, to be the owner or boss is to rule and control by directives. Look at the following list. Note carefully the contrast between what the world says and what the kingdom says.

WHAT THE WORLD SAYS	WHAT THE KINGDOM SAYS
Pride is important.	Humility is essential.
Hitch your wagon to a star.	Jesus is Lord.
Success	Obedience
Professionalism	Servanthood
Competition	Service
Maintain your rights.	Give all your rights to God.
Negotiate for the best deal.	Obey God's commands.
Excellence	Christlikeness
Save your life.	Lose your life for my sake.
Affirm self.	Deny self.
Accomplishments	Character
You don't have to take that.	Take up your cross.
Live to die.	Die to live.
Rule and be served.	Serve in order to rule.
Things will make you happy.	Godly character brings joy.
Walk by sight.	Walk by faith.
Set long-range goals.	God reveals the future.
Take the initiative.	Let God take the initiative.
Get revenge.	Do good to your persecutors.
Eat, drink, and be merry.	Seek first the kingdom of God.

The man God uses must be kingdom-oriented. In his letter to the Galatians, Paul said, "God forbid that I should boast except in the cross of our Lord Jesus Christ, by whom the world has been crucified to me, and I to the world" (Gal. 6:14 NKJV). Paul was the leading missionary to the Gentiles, a man of great faith and stamina, who had endured prison, beatings, stonings, and whippings, all without dishonoring God. Yet, he said, "God forbid that I should boast, except in the cross of our Lord Jesus Christ."

The cross was crucial to Paul's ministry and to Paul's understanding of who he was and who God is. Paul was humbled by the fact that the only significant, lasting thing about him grew out of the execution that marked the sacrifice of the Savior. But what was rated a failure in the world's eyes represented eternal life for that same world. The last verses of Acts record Paul's life passion. Acts 28:30–31 lets us know that Paul remained committed to the kingdom of God even at the end of his life.

> "FOR TWO WHOLE YEARS PAUL STAYED THERE IN HIS OWN RENTED HOUSE AND WELCOMED ALL WHO CAME TO SEE HIM. BOLDLY AND WITHOUT HINDRANCE HE PREACHED THE KINGDOM OF GOD AND TAUGHT ABOUT THE LORD JESUS CHRIST"
> (ACTS 28:30–31)

Having been transformed through a relationship with God through faith in Jesus Christ, such a man's mind, heart, will, and life belong to Jesus Christ alone. He has been reoriented to God and God's kingdom. He is now convinced that in Christ he is filled with "all the fullness of God" (Eph. 3:19).

In the life of the man God uses, this means:

▸ "God is able to make all grace abound to you, so that in all things at all times, having all that you need, you will abound in every good work" (2 Cor. 9:8).

▸ "No matter how many promises God has made, they are 'Yes' in Christ. And so through him the 'Amen' is spoken by us to the glory of God" (2 Cor. 1:20).

▸ "God will meet all your needs according to his glorious riches in Christ Jesus" (Phil. 4:19).

▸ If he has "'faith as small as a mustard seed .... Nothing will be impossible'" (Matt. 17:20) for him.

▸ "'If you remain in me and my words remain in you, ask whatever you wish, and it will be given you'" (John 15:7).

Numerous promises are ours as children of God working together with God in the workplace, at home, in his church, and throughout the world!

The man God uses is one who has absolute, unconditional trust, reliance, and faith in God. He is a man through whom God can do all things "exceedingly abundantly above all that we ask or think" (Eph. 3:20 NKJV). He lives with a clear, God-given sense of direction. He knows the ways of God in the world. His heart is set with the awareness of the awesome consequences of being sent by God. The presence of God is with him expressing himself just as God promised.

Therefore, the man God uses keeps his character with integrity, knowing that his life is a highway for God to work in every place God chooses to place him. Nothing is impossible through his life!

What incredible changes and blessings can flow through the man God uses (2 Cor. 5:17–20). Unstable families he touches can find refuge in Christ through him (Ps. 46:1). Those broken in spirit can be made whole in Christ through him (Luke 4:18–19). Many can come to understand and experience the certain will of God for their lives and circumstances because of his faithful sharing. Conflicts can be resolved and reconciliation realized through the power of the Lord through him (Matt. 5:9). Significant decisions can be made, because in his life are all the wisdom and knowledge of God (Col. 2:2–3; James 1:5), and many can come to saving faith in Jesus Christ.

Can you grasp the meaning of being a man God uses? It causes me to stand in awe and trembling, knowing who I am as a child of God, knowing who has sent me to be changed and to be an instrument of change in others' lives—especially those who do not know God.

The man God uses is committed to the cost involved in following God. He has confidence in the Holy Spirit to take him through every circumstance. There will be conflict and opposition in the process of walking with the Lord. But there will be no cost he will encounter that the Holy Spirit will not empower him to work through.

The man God uses seeks a Spirit-filled life (Eph. 5:18) and displays the fruit of the Spirit (Gal. 5:22–25). Such a life cannot be explained by the world around him but will be used of God to be light in the man's world (Eph. 5:8–10).

The man God uses does not pattern his life after well-known military strategists, political figures, heroes of this world, or other prominent Christians. Rather, he makes an absolute commitment to pattern his life after Jesus Christ as the Master Servant.

> "THE CENTRAL THING ABOUT THE KINGDOM OF
> JESUS CHRIST IS A PERSONAL RELATIONSHIP TO
> HIMSELF, NOT PUBLIC USEFULNESS TO MEN."[2]
> —OSWALD CHAMBERS

LIVE IN FAITH

I remember encouraging several Christian teachers in a public high school to "speak the truth in love" to the principal about several issues. We prayed, God heard our prayers, and he honored the witness of the teachers. In time, significant, God-honoring changes were made in the curriculum and in the graduation program.

Our church also encouraged men who were working for an oil company refinery to request not to work on Sunday in order to honor their Lord and lead their families. Never before had such a request been made. As a church, we prayed for them and their witness.

The men made their request, and it was granted without question. God was honored, families were strengthened, and the men realized the difference their lives could make in the workplace. It set a clear example for others and for their own children of what it means to live in faith.

In John 4:10, Jesus was clearly speaking a completely different language from the Samaritan woman he met at Jacob's well. She was talking about the water from the well, and Jesus was talking about "living water." She talked of worshiping God on a mountain; Christ talked of worshiping in spirit and truth (John 4:21–24). She talked about the Messiah, and Christ told her it was he of whom she spoke (John 4:25–26).

At this point she and Christ could see eye to eye. Her reaction was to run into the town to bring back everyone who would listen to her (John 4:28–29). Her life was changed! Her belief in Christ allowed her to see clearly for the first time from a kingdom perspective. So many people of her city were changed that they urged Jesus to stay two more days with them, and many more believed because of it!

We try to teach evangelism to Christians, or how to witness as kingdom citizens. Evangelism is not a program. It is a byproduct of a healthy, growing, vibrant relationship with Jesus Christ as Lord. Men who walk in a dynamic relationship with Christ witness by nature and draw persons to him. Jesus did not have to teach the woman at the well how to witness. He redeemed her, and she brought the whole city to see the man who changed her life!

FORGIVENESS AND RECONCILIATION

When the man God uses becomes God-oriented, he sees his life as a kingdom citizen and reflects God's nature to others. This is most evident in the area of forgiveness. The world knows little of the real meaning of forgiveness because it has never known God's forgiveness.

Jesus told his disciples how to treat their enemies. They must love them, pray for them, do good to them, and bless them (Matt.

5:43—44). The world cannot do this, but a Christian can, because he is enabled by Jesus living through him.

Jesus instructed his disciples not only to forgive others but also to demonstrate a lifestyle of forgiveness to others. Jesus told his disciples to forgive everyone 490 times or 70 times 7 (Matt. 18:21—22). Those who follow Jesus must forgive as he would. His goal is to break down barriers and reach people, not to set up barriers through hatred, resentment, bearing grudges, or retribution. None of these will help bring others to Christ. They will only drive people further away and compromise any witness believers might otherwise have with them. Christ's followers are to be used of God to draw people by love and love alone.

Paul explained in 2 Corinthians 5:17—20 that when we were born from above we were made into new creatures and God gave us the ministry of reconciliation. Paul said that believers are workers together with God (2 Cor. 6:1—2 NKJV) in the process of reconciliation.

Think of how many marriages could be healed, how many children could be restored, and how many churches could be brought together in love. Think of the resolution of conflict that could come to the workplaces of the nation! Think of the sorrow that could be averted and brokenness prevented as godly men live in the power of the Holy Spirit!

Jim faced a difficult crisis as God's servant. He worked as a chaplain in a youth prison. During a guards' strike, the police were called in to take over guard duties. But soon the police had lost control, and riots broke out in three units.

The prison staff allowed Jim to cross the picket line to assess the situation because they trusted his integrity. They agreed to do whatever Jim thought best. After much prayer, Jim entered the prison. The police directed him to a small unit for the most hardened and violent criminals.

> A GODLY MAN WILL AT ALL TIMES BE READY TO BE INVOLVED IN RECONCILIATION WHETHER WITH COWORKERS, HIS WIFE, HIS CHILDREN, HIS FRIENDS, OR IN HIS CHURCH.

Jim walked into the unit and said firmly, "Clean out your cells and in you go." Much to his amazement, they did! With fear he went into the next unit where the riot was well underway. As he walked in, the leader—a 6' 4", 240 lb. weightlifter—came running up to him yelling, "Get me out of here!" Jim opened his cell, and in he went. The riot was over!

Jim informed the staff that they did not need to enter with force. He explained later that he felt the presence of the Prince of Peace with him that day. Christians are able to be highways over which the love and compassion of Christ can flow. "A highway will be there; it will be called the Way of Holiness. The unclean will not journey on it; it will be for those who walk in that Way; wicked fools will not go about on it" (Isa. 35:8). God is able to fill you with his Holy Spirit and enable you to be a "highway for God"!

FAITH

Among the advantages of the man God uses are the incredible possibilities available through faith in God. As kingdom citizens, we are promised that faith accesses the power of God in all circumstances. Faith can take on different forms, depending on the situation. This is because faith is a confident expectation concerning your relationship with God (Heb. 11:1), and God never changes, regardless of circumstances. When a man truly knows God and fully trusts him, his focus shifts from self and circumstance to God and relationship.

Essentially, faith is believing that what you see as reality from a human standpoint is inaccurate. Faith sees a kingdom reality of what God wants to happen in and through your life.

Hebrews 11:32–40 references examples of people God used. Those who let God accomplish mighty things through them did so because they believed he would. Those who were able to withstand tremendous persecution, opposition, and even death did so according to their faith in the one who could keep them in his love for eternity. "This is the victory that has overcome the world, even our faith" (1 John 5:4).

What God says is true to you. The Holy Spirit living in you bears witness to God's Word. You can base your life on all God says in his Word. God says he loves you and laid down his life for you. You can always be confident about God's love for you, regardless of the circumstances. You don't have to be blown about by your circumstances. If you lose your job, for example, God's love for you will keep you steady. Your family will see your faith in God and they, too, will feel secure.

God is faithful, and all his promises are true. You can search out the promises of God in the Bible and, with confidence, live by them. The promises in verses such as Hebrews 13:5, Matthew 28:20, and Philippians 4:19 are just a few of God's assurances that he will never leave you, is with you always, and shall supply all of your needs. These promises can shape our lives and give us confidence as kingdom citizens.

Because God has given you promises in his Word, you can, with great confidence in God's unfailing presence and provision, live your life boldly before a watching and hurting world. Everyone may forsake you, even your family and friends, but this will not destroy you, for you know God's promises! You know God has not, nor will he ever, leave you or forsake you. Others who watch you will be amazed at your faith and will be attracted to the God you serve. Your testimony of God's faithfulness will draw them.

You can also have faith in God's provision for you. God's promises reveal that: (1) nothing is impossible for him to do in and through your life, and (2) "God shall supply all your need according to His riches in glory by Christ Jesus" (Phil. 4:19 NKJV).

Knowing and believing this, you can turn to God to meet your every need. Your life of faith will be a testimony to your family, friends, and fellow workers as they see your loving heavenly Father taking care of you according to your faith in his promises.

Our ultimate goal should be to allow Christ complete freedom in our lives (Gal. 2:20)—to be so completely dependent on Christ, through faith, that he can shine through us to a desperate and needy world.

George Müller began moving through life as a thief, liar, and scoundrel. By the age of sixteen, he was imprisoned for unpaid debts. Once freed, through deceit and forgery, he traveled about the country and completed his university studies on other people's money.

However, when he received Christ as his Savior, George Müller was changed by God's presence in his life. He began to demonstrate an amazing faith in God. Müller opened an orphanage in England in April 1836, and by the next year two more orphanages were opened. By the end of his life, several new orphanages were constructed and thousands of orphans cared for.

The amazing fact about Müller is how he managed his orphan ministry. He relied completely on private prayer for God to provide food, clothing, and every item for maintaining his orphanages and caring for his charges. Never once did his children go without clothing or food. The food may have come just after the dinner prayer was said, but it was always on time. He refused any salary and never asked for money. He dedicated his life to showing that God's Word is true, "God shall supply all your need according to His riches in glory by Christ Jesus" (Phil. 4:19 NKJV). "Without faith it is impossible to please God, because anyone who comes to him must believe that he exists and that he rewards those who earnestly seek him" (Heb. 11:6).

SEEK FIRST HIS KINGDOM

As kingdom citizens we are aware of the God who is near and of his resources. We go from an encounter with God to the trenches—from the mountaintop into the valley. We ask God to take our spiritual encounter with him and apply it to our practical situations.

A congregation in Modesto, California, prayed that God would invite them to join his activity in their neighborhood. One thing that was apparent to everyone was the growing population of Eastern Indians in the area. The congregation's pastor, Mike Atinsky, was dining out when a Hindu woman asked him if she had understood correctly that he was a minister. After a brief conversation, she asked him to tell her about Jesus. Later she became a Christian and joined Mike's congregation, even though it was not close to her home. Through her becoming a Christian, the pastor was introduced to her son and daughter-in-law. They subsequently heard and believed the gospel and also became Christians. They lived in the neighborhood of the church and were apparently part of God's provision for involving the congregation in his activity. God led the couple to begin a ministry to Eastern Indians in their home. This led to an Eastern Indian congregation, all as the result of believers' praying and trusting God to lead them.[3]

> "AND A HIGHWAY WILL BE THERE;
>   IT WILL BE CALLED THE WAY OF HOLINESS.
> THE UNCLEAN WILL NOT JOURNEY ON IT;
>   IT WILL BE FOR THOSE WHO WALK IN THAT
>   WAY;
>   WICKED FOOLS WILL NOT GO ABOUT ON IT."
>
> (ISA. 35:8)

One of the most radical revelations Christ made about himself is found in John 14:6, "'I am the way and the truth and the life. No one comes to the Father except through me.'" In this verse, Jesus didn't say, I'll show you the way, or I know the truth and will tell it to you, or I can heal you and give you a better life. Rather, he said that he is the way, the truth, and the life.

When Christ is present, the truth of every situation differs from purely human perceptions. Take, for example, the disciples enduring a storm on the Sea of Galilee as they accompanied Jesus.

Jesus fell asleep in the boat. A sudden and ferocious storm arose. To the disciples' human understanding, taking into account the nature of the storm in comparison to the ability of their vessel, they were certain they would begin sinking soon. They were frantic! But the truth of the situation was not that they would sink. The Truth of the situation was asleep in the boat! The reality of Christ's presence made, and makes, all the difference. "Then he got up and rebuked the winds and the waves, and it was completely calm" (Matt. 8:26).

> "CARRY EACH OTHER'S BURDENS, AND IN THIS WAY
> YOU WILL FULFILL THE LAW OF CHRIST."
> (GAL. 6:2)

What was the truth in the death of Lazarus as recorded in John 11? From the world's perspective, not only was Jesus' friend Lazarus dead, but his body had begun to decompose. From the world's perspective, there was no hope. But when the Truth arrived, he commanded, "'Lazarus, come out!'" and his resurrected friend stepped forth. Did the presence of Christ make a difference in the truth of the situation? You bet it did!

How about those who had been blind or lame since birth and were made whole by Christ? From the world's perspective, their situations were hopeless. But in Christ, in Truth, the reality of the situation was completely opposite. They were not only able to see and to walk, but they could now more effectively proclaim the glory of Christ to a watching, astonished world.

According to Christ's disciples, the truth of the situation dictated that they ought to send the thousands of people away to the towns and villages to buy food after a long day of listening to the Master (Matt. 14). After all, the only food they could find was a few small fish and a couple of loaves of bread. Was the truth that the people would starve? No.

When Truth spoke, the reality of the situation became dramatically different. More than five thousand were fed, and twelve baskets of leftover bread were collected. Kingdom realities rarely mesh with the world's reality.

How can you possibly know the truth of any situation without checking first with the real Truth? You can't. The world's perspective on any situation is suspect because the world does not understand the truth, and neither will the world understand your faith in Christ who is Truth.

> YOU CAN NEVER REALLY KNOW THE TRUTH OF THE SITUATION UNTIL YOU'VE CHECKED WITH THE ONE WHO IS TRUTH.

When my daughter was diagnosed with cancer at age sixteen, our human nature saw the truth as a devastating reality leading to death. Then we inquired from the one who is Truth. He spoke from a kingdom reality, one not limited to our laws of nature, time, or space. He revealed to us, just as he had to the sisters of Lazarus, that it was not a sickness leading to death but that through it he would be glorified. We clung to the Truth as revealed to us. We prayed fervently and asked many others to pray for us on behalf of our sick daughter. And God was faithful to his promises to us. Others in the same condition died. But according to God's plan for my daughter, she lives. It was important for us to seek reality from the only one who knows the truth of every situation. You will never know the truth of any situation until you've sought Christ and his will for your life.

In closing, let me speak to married men. Your marriage, at first glance, may seem at a hopeless impasse headed for destruction. But when you seek the living Christ in the middle of your relationship, things begin to take on a different perspective. If you feel your marriage is no match for God, you don't know the Almighty God of the Bible or the awesome God whose kingdom continues to go forth today. In fact, maybe that's the heart of your marriage problem. You have not allowed God to be an integral part of your relationship. Christ will change your marriage into something wonderful and exciting if he is allowed his way with you. Men, your marriage is your single most important priority after your relationship with Christ. It is more important than your relationship with your children, your parents, your job, your hobbies, or any other thing in your life. God will honor the covenant you made with your wife before him on your wedding day. He will guide you safely out of the stormy waters to safe harbors.

THE KINGDOM IS WHERE YOU ARE

The kingdom is where you are—in your family, your workplace, your church, your nation, and your world.

THE KINGDOM IN YOUR FAMILY

One of the most important aspects of a man's life is his role as a kingdom citizen in the home. If fathers are ever to be the godly men their families need, they must regularly seek the Lord. The impact a father has on his children will last the rest of their lives. The leadership and love a husband shows his wife is critical to the spiritual stability and effectiveness of his wife and marriage. The man God uses, in terms of his spiritual life and his faithful obedience to God, serves as a model for his wife and children.

I once was asked by a parent to speak to the teenage children who were not Christians. In talking with the teens, I learned that they were not convinced of their father's conversion. They brought up several corrupt activities he had been involved in before and after he was saved. They saw no need to take God seriously because they didn't see their father doing so. This father did not realize that, although he had given his life to Christ, he had not acted toward his children in a way to draw them to the Christ He now served. His children needed to see the incredible difference Christ makes in fathers when they are changed from the inside out by the power of the Holy Spirit.

> "THEREFORE CONFESS YOUR SINS TO EACH OTHER AND PRAY FOR EACH OTHER SO THAT YOU MAY BE HEALED. THE PRAYER OF A RIGHTEOUS MAN IS POWERFUL AND EFFECTIVE."
> (JAMES 5:16)

One man, saved out of a wealthy, partying lifestyle, prayed for his wife for years. Each time we would meet together as men, he asked for prayer for her. She was not ready to give up the lifestyle she was accustomed to and resented her husband's religion. After years of experiencing her husband's prayer, love, and Christlike behavior, her attitude softened. She allowed her young children to go to church and began attending herself. It wasn't long before her husband told us she had accepted Christ. We all rejoiced with him. Christ is now the center of their marriage and family life. They are able to serve together and demonstrate the kingdom through their home life.

Read Galatians 6:2. Could you benefit from prayers for your family? Do you believe other men could benefit from your prayers for their homes? Pause now and pray, both for those God would use to carry your burdens with you and those you could serve by praying and caring for them.

If you are the only believer in your family, you will be tested by those who are not. They will want to see if your commitment to Christ is genuine. They will want to know if you will "grow out of it" or if it is just a "passing phase." Persevere. Remain faithful in both your silent and verbal witness to them. Love them as Christ would. Treat them with utmost care. Pray without ceasing for God to reclaim their souls from the world that they might experience the joy of his salvation. Invite other Christians to pray with you specifically for your family members as well as for your positive testimony as you live with them. God honors the prayers of those whose hearts belong to him.

Read James 5:16. This verse is an encouragement because it is one of God's promises. Close your eyes and say it to yourself.

THE KINGDOM IN YOUR WORKPLACE

Wherever God's people are, they bring with them the power of God to change lives and circumstances. All God's people in all places at all times in God's way can radically impact their workplace with his power and Spirit. Remember the apostle Paul's words, "For to me, to live is Christ and to die is gain" (Phil. 1:21) and "I have been crucified with Christ and I no longer live, but Christ lives in me" (Gal. 2:20). Christ will work through you as you allow him to, using you in the ordinary circumstances of your job to make an extraordinary impact in your workplace!

Remember, God has placed us with his purposes in mind. We are to seek God's will for our vocations and to look for his activity in our workplaces. Seeing God at work where we are is exciting, and watching him work through us to bring hope and redemption to those with whom we work is thrilling. Remember who lives in you and goes with you to work. You are carrying inside you the same power and the same person that raised Christ from the dead, calmed the storming sea, healed the blind, and pummeled Satan's forces into submission.

THE KINGDOM IN YOUR CHURCH

There is no better place to see the kingdom of God at work than in the local church. Christ says, "'I will build my church, and the gates of [Hell] will not overcome it'" (Matt. 16:18). The kingdom of God cannot be destroyed. The church, as Christ's body, can accomplish amazing feats as it follows his leadership and moves according to his ways. In his book *The Body*, Charles Colson shares incident after incident where the church united brought down stronghold after stronghold and has made an impact on entire nations because of Christ's power flowing through it.

If the church stays focused on God's will and God's ways, nothing can stop it from accomplishing his purposes in its communities, towns, and cities. When the church's focus is drawn away from Christ, it begins to become ineffective and divided and may even close its doors for good. The man God uses will serve through his church to help it stay on course and remain dependent on the Holy Spirit for equipping and guidance and on Christ for his power to accomplish what he intends the church to do.

What areas in your church has the Holy Spirit been speaking to you about? How does he want you to invest your life in a ministry of your church to help it stay focused and on track?

THE KINGDOM IN YOUR NATION AND YOUR WORLD

If God has unconditional rights to your life, then you will accept that he has the right to send you anywhere, at anytime, for his purposes. I once asked a congregation if they believed this to be true. "Amen" rang out from every corner of the auditorium. Then I asked how many of them had valid passports! Only a few nervous chuckles could be heard in response. Their actions indicated more about what they believed than their words.

God is actively at work in your nation and around the world. He may need someone of your caliber and qualifications for a special task in a country that will not permit missionaries. You may be the only one who could go to be his "highway of holiness."

A passport may not be the only thing that will keep you from being sent by God; it could be your mounting debt. Christians who owe so much to so many will find it more difficult to be available for God's use. The man God uses must depend on God for his needs and must not be seduced by credit. Satan can use large debts to compromise otherwise useful men and place them in bondage to their creditors.

God has opportunities for godly men all around the world, but only a handful are prepared to go. "'For many are called, but few are chosen'" (Matt. 22:14 NKJV). The man God uses will not allow himself to be in bondage to anything and will be free to go at a moment's notice wherever God will send him. It will not matter to him if it be to the next neighborhood or to the farthest continent.

HOW TO RESPOND TO GOD'S ACTIVITY

We are to watch for God to reveal to us what he is doing. God's revelation to us is his invitation to join him in his activity. This may seem backward to some people. They prefer to start their own activity for God and then ask him to come and join them!

Christ did only what the Father showed him to do, nothing more and nothing less. "'My Father has been working until now, and I have been working.'" "'Most assuredly, I say to you, the Son can do nothing of Himself, but what He sees the Father do; for whatever He does, the Son also does in like manner. For the Father loves the Son, and shows Him all things that He Himself does'" (John 5:17, 19–20 NKJV).

Christ is our example and model. We must pattern our lives after his relationship with the Father and follow Christ's pattern of relating to the Father.

God's main purpose is to reconcile a lost world to himself. God always works from his kingdom perspective with eternity in mind. It is important for us to know what God is up to in our lives, our families, our workplaces, our nation, and our world. The Holy Spirit will show you when you ask him.

THINK ABOUT—PRAY ABOUT

When God shows you his activity and his plans, you must choose to join him or be disobedient. Each time you join God he uses you to impact eternity, and you grow in faith and character.

▸ Each time you are disobedient, you face the consequences of your actions, and God will patiently begin to bring you back on track again. Even though God will not give up on you and will continue to shape and mold you, you may have lost an opportunity to serve him that will not come again. Pray and commit to be the man God uses in all areas of your life.

▸ Ask God to help you understand the impact of truth on building God's kingdom. Ask God to show you how you can be used by living out truth in your life and world. Don't worry about what men can do, but be absolutely concerned about what God can do. The kingdom-oriented man will not fear men but will have a healthy sense of awe and fear of God. He will be confident God will vindicate him for his glory. Pray a prayer of praise and thanksgiving to God for your relationship with him.

▸ Is living by faith a foreign concept to you, or is it something you are able to practice regularly? Think about some of the areas in which you completely depend on God. If what you have thought of is limited to crisis situations, or things out of your control, you may want to consider the blessings you may be missing. Pray about depending more on God in other areas of your life.

‣ God still calms the storms in life for those who truly seek him. Pray today about those areas of your life where God can calm the storm. Seek first his kingdom and grow in your relationship with God.

---

1. J. Hudson Taylor as quoted by Warren W. Wiersbe, *Victorious Christians You Should Know* (Grand Rapids: Baker Book House, 1984), 12.

2. Oswald Chambers, *My Utmost for His Highest* (Uhrichsville, Ohio: Barbour and Company, Inc.), 293.

3. "A New Ministry to Hindus in California," *Experiencing God REPORT* (September 1996), 4.

Chapter 7

ON MISSION WITH GOD IN OUR WORLD

As God's fellow workers we urge you not to receive
God's grace in vain.

—2 Corinthians 6:1

T hroughout this book and especially in this final chapter, we have sought and will seek to present from the Scriptures "God's ideal" for his people. You may be tempted to see God's ideal, look at your life or your church, and become somewhat discouraged. Don't! Anyone who believes God and sets about to help God's people become God's best will always experience the full resources of God at work through him to bring it to pass. Set your hearts and lives to be God's fellow workers, and do not "receive God's grace in vain" (2 Cor. 6:1). "Let us not become weary in doing good, for at the proper time we will reap a harvest if we do not give up" (Gal. 6:9). God is moving mightily in his people, for his purposes, even today.

GOD'S PEOPLE

Throughout Scripture, God's focus is always on his people. Through his people God will bring a lost world to himself. In 1904, revival began to sweep the Welsh region of the United Kingdom. God chose to use Evan Roberts in a special way. Roberts and others brought revival to the remotest parts of Wales. Within five months 100,000 people found Christ and joined churches. Taverns went bankrupt, crime stopped, and communities were changed.[1]

Revival isn't an evangelistic appeal; it is God's people getting right with God and then having an impact on their communities. When the people of Wales took seriously their relationship to God, the Holy Spirit was freed to sweep across their nation with incredible power and effect.[2]

That is God's pattern. Jesus said that when the Father is glorified the ruler of this world (Satan) is driven out. Jesus also said, "'I, when I am lifted up from the earth, will draw all men to myself'" (John 12:32).

When God's people demonstrate his life-changing power in their lives, the world will not only take notice but will also be uncontrollably drawn to Christ by the power of the presence of God. "'No one can come to me unless the Father who sent me draws him, and I will raise him up at the last day. It is written in the Prophets: "They will all be taught by God." Everyone who listens to the Father and learns from him comes to me'" (John 6:44—45).

God draws unbelievers to himself using his people as agents of light reflecting his glory. This is the main purpose of God's people, to be used by his power working through them to draw others to Christ.

THE MAN GOD USES

Throughout this book we have seen God's pattern for using a man:

▸ God chooses a man when he sees a heart ready to be used and character that comes from a clean, pure, right relationship with him.

▸ God calls that man through his Word, his people, his Spirit, or circumstances. Then God confirms his call to that man through the church.

▸ God prepares a man, shaping and molding him for God's purposes in the world. God orients him for special times and for kingdom purposes.

▸ God uses the man he has chosen, called, and prepared by taking that man on mission with him to accomplish God's purposes.

Where are you, personally, in God's "process"? Where are the men in your church or your workplace? Has God indicated he is ready to take you and them with him on his mission to redeem lost souls?

GOD HAS ASKED YOU TO BE HIS PEOPLE

God purposed to create a people for himself. "Then Moses went up to God, and the LORD called to him from the mountain and said, 'This is what you are to say to the house of Jacob and what you are to tell the people of Israel: "You yourselves have seen what I did to Egypt, and how I carried you on eagles' wings and brought you to myself. Now if you obey me fully and keep my covenant, then out of all nations you will be my treasured possession. Although the whole earth is mine, you will be for me a kingdom of priests and a holy nation"'" (Exod. 19:3–6).

> "BUT YOU ARE A CHOSEN PEOPLE, A ROYAL PRIEST-
> HOOD, A HOLY NATION, A PEOPLE BELONGING TO
> GOD, THAT YOU MAY DECLARE THE PRAISES OF HIM
> WHO CALLED YOU OUT OF DARKNESS INTO HIS
> WONDERFUL LIGHT. ONCE YOU WERE NOT A
> PEOPLE, BUT NOW YOU ARE THE PEOPLE OF GOD;
> ONCE YOU HAD NOT RECEIVED MERCY, BUT NOW
> YOU HAVE RECEIVED MERCY."
> (1 Pet. 2:9–10)

When God intersected the lives of the people of Israel, they became a treasured possession, a kingdom of priests, a holy nation. But they were fearful of God and hesitant to respond directly to his invitation to become his covenant people. They insisted that Moses go to God on their behalf rather than having God speak directly to them (Exod. 20:19). Rather than coming before God as a kingdom of priests, they sent Moses to act as a priest for them.

God's people settled for a secondhand relationship with God, which brings little motivation toward service or accountability. God wanted to use a people belonging to himself, that praise him and know that they have received mercy (1 Pet. 2:9–10).

God planned from before time to create a people he could love and who would love him back for eternity. Man's sin broke that love relationship and brought eternal separation from God. But through the atoning sacrifice of Christ, the covenant love relationship was reestablished through faith in Jesus Christ and obedience to his Word. God uses our faith as the means by which we have access to him once again.

God continues to create a faithful generation of people through whom he can work to redeem a lost world to himself. As each generation passes away, a new one is born that must place its faith and trust in the Creator. Christ said that his "Father is always at his work to this very day" (John 5:17). God is at work creating a people to use for his kingdom purposes. All those who have placed their faith in Christ and turned their lives over for his use are a part of God's kingdom.

God's people are to be to him a "kingdom of priests," a "royal priesthood." God created a people for himself to perform some important duties. God's people serve him as a kingdom of royal priests. The role of God's priests is significant. The Old Testament shows the development of God's priests as mediators between God and man (Lev. 22:1). Their primary function was handling sacrifices to God on behalf of the people. They were to minister to the people in God's name and help the people know how to come acceptably before God and fulfill their religious duties.

They also were to interpret God's will to the people and go to God on their behalf seeking his wisdom. When Christ died on the cross, he fulfilled all the required sacrifices for sin, once and for all. We no longer must go through a human mediator to gain access to God; we go through Christ. As he sacrificed his body, we too are called to offer our bodies as a living sacrifice, holy and acceptable to God (Rom. 12:1).

We are to act as ambassadors for God to those who live without him. We are to bring his message of hope, "as though God were making his appeal through us" (2 Cor. 5:18–20), to those who do not call Jesus Christ Lord.

As God's priests and holy nation, we have the truth and the light as a part of our very nature. As Christians we bear witness to others of the truth of Christ residing in us. Sometimes all we have to do is lead people into the presence of God, and God will do the rest.

A pastor told me of a young man who called him and asked if he might bring his girlfriend by the church. When the two arrived, the girlfriend was blindfolded and did not know where she was. In fact, she thought they were going out for dinner to a secret restaurant! The pastor followed the two as the young man led his girlfriend up onto the sanctuary platform, stood her before the cross on the wall, then removed the blindfold. At once she shrieked and fell to her knees sobbing. The story unfolded that the young man was leaving the country for a long time and knew his girlfriend was not right with God. He wanted her to settle things spiritually before he left.

When we are brought before the presence of God, his Holy Spirit can do mighty works in our lives and in the lives of others who are confronted with their sin.

Sometimes going to people on behalf of God is difficult. I remember sharing God's Word with a man who was committing adultery and who planned to leave his wife and children. Confronting the sinful situation, I pleaded with him to repent. I spoke of the dire consequences he and his family would face should he continue, but he remained undeterred.

The prophet Nathan had to confront David with his sin and could have lost his life for doing so. John the Baptist also faced the wrath of Herod after rebuking him in his fornication. Paul and Silas were thrown in prison, beaten, and whipped several times for bringing God's message of salvation to the lost. Even the school board chairman (from earlier in this book) was slandered, verbally abused, and harassed for bringing his Christian convictions into his decisions. Sometimes, as God's priests, we must bear the insults that Christ faced, and we must endure the pain of rejection as Christ did. Christ's advice to those who follow him is not to fear those who can harm them physically and to remember that whoever acknowledges him before others will be acknowledged by him before the heavenly Father (Matt. 10:24–25, 28, 32–33).

WE ARE INTERCESSORS

As God's people, one of our responsibilities is to be intercessors. Christians are intercessors to God for those in need of his grace and intervention in their lives. We seek to intervene in the lives of those around us to make a spiritual difference in the direction they are heading.

There is a way that leads to life. "'Wide is the gate and broad is the road that leads to destruction, and many enter through it. But small is the gate and narrow the road that leads to life, and only a few find it'" (Matt. 7:13–14). We share an urgency with Christ to communicate that truth to those heading down the road to destruction!

Intercession is no small task for the man God uses. Even though it can be a wearisome, time-consuming effort, the rewards are tremendous. Souls are saved, lives are changed, sick people are healed, jobs are found, families are reunited, relationships are restored, people are released from prison, barriers are removed, and the work of the devil is thwarted. In essence, the miraculous becomes a regular occurrence as the result of intercession. People others had long since given up on have come to saving faith in Christ because someone persevered in faithful intercession for them. When God's people come together, God's power and action are released to accomplish what he wills. Our prayers allow us to become more aware of how God wants to use us.

> THE MIRACULOUS BECOMES A REGULAR OCCUR-
> RENCE AS THE RESULT OF INTERCESSION.

David Grant, a doctor who belonged to a racquetball club, had no idea that his new racquetball partner was leading a double life. At the club, Bill Fay was the brash corporate climber. In reality, he also had a sideline in crime. All the doctor knew was that this man didn't know Christ.

David befriended, witnessed to, and prayed for Bill. When the doctor saw Bill's arrest on the evening news, he was more certain than ever that God had placed this man in his life for a purpose. As every sordid detail came out about Bill, David stayed available. And when Bill reached the end of his rope, he turned to a minister who led him to Christ. Bill called his friend, David, because he knew that the one who prayed for him throughout their relationship would rejoice with him now. Bill Fay entered the ministry and has served

God as an evangelist, not only witnessing for Christ but also teaching hundreds of thousands how to witness, for nearly twenty years. A multitude of people have heard, responded to, and obeyed the gospel, not only because of Bill's devotion to God but also because David Grant interceded for Bill.[3]

WE ARE WORSHIPERS

As God's kingdom of priests, we are facilitators of worship before him. Worship is giving God praise, adoration, glory, honor, devotion, and love. It is an encounter with God where there is total submission to God. Unfortunately, some Christians have developed the idea that worship is for the worshiper rather than for God. They look to see what they are getting out of worship rather than what they are bringing to a holy God in worship.

The attitudes we are to bring to our worship are described in God's Word. "Love the LORD your God with all your heart and with all your soul and with all your strength" (Deut. 6:5). "If you are offering your gift at the altar and there remember that your brother has something against you, leave your gift there in front of the altar. First go and be reconciled to your brother; then come and offer your gift" (Matt. 5:23–24).

Worship is first and foremost a heart attitude. We can expect to miss meeting God if we come with pride, sin, anger, an unrepentant spirit, or neglect in our relationship with him. When our approach to God is right, then our intellect, emotions, and senses come together for a glorious meeting with God through Christ. The prophet Micah asked the question,

> "With what shall I come before the Lord
>   and bow down before the exalted God?

> Shall I come before him with burnt offerings,
>   with calves a year old?
> Will the LORD be pleased with thousands of rams,
>   with ten thousand rivers of oil?
> Shall I offer my firstborn for my transgression,
>   the fruit of my body for the sin of my soul?"

(Mic. 6:6–7)

Micah answers these questions with what is acceptable and pleasing to God in worship,

> "He has showed you, O man, what is good.
>   And what does the LORD require of you?
> To act justly and to love mercy
>   and to walk humbly with your God."

(Mic. 6:8)

Worship is both personal and corporate. We are a people belonging to God, and we function best in community together. God has even given us instructions for his worship that grow out of our relationship with him, our relationship with other believers, and the knowledge that when we relate to other believers we are indeed relating to him, as well! So God requires that we gather together. "Let us not give up meeting together, as some are in the habit of doing, but let us encourage one another" (Heb. 10:25).

Proclaiming God's truth, with words and music, along with giving thanks to God are elements God requires. "Speak to one another with psalms, hymns and spiritual songs. Sing and make music in your heart to the Lord, always giving thanks to God the

Father for everything, in the name of our Lord Jesus Christ" (Eph. 5:19–20).

Even as God has given us his commands for the attitude and expressions he desires in worship, he also desires to be the central focus of our worship. Giving God glory is not accomplished with inner or outer confusion. "God is not a God of disorder but of peace" (1 Cor. 14:33).

One of the roles the man God uses can play is to identify and correct man-centered worship. Like most good things, there are counterfeits in worship that do not bring people before God in an acceptable fashion. People leave entertained and motivated, but they have not tasted the Living Waters. People may have been startled by how different or unique the experience was, but they may not have come away with the words of life. In fact, true worship may leave you broken, repentant, and sorrowful— quite the opposite of the hype some have brought inside the church walls.

God will refuse to accept worship that is halfhearted or less than what he deserves. Worship that requires little of us is like-wise worth little to God. Evaluate your own worship. Does your worship experience end at the close of the service, or are you usually motivated to change or take action because of your encounter with God?

Intercession and worship are two elements of service on mis-sion with God in our world. Intercession allows us to represent God to others. In the corporate experience of worship, individual lives will be changed by the impact of the Holy Spirit. The man God uses functions through intercession and worship in a corpo-rate body of believers with Christ as the Head of the body.

THE BODY OF CHRIST

Many people know the church is the body of Christ but have no idea how that body functions. They may have some vague concept that the body of Christ should evangelize the world, feed the hungry, clothe the down-and-out, or meet together regularly to worship, but they don't know how they are to function within the body.

God places the men he uses into bodies of believers for particular reasons. Just our acceptance of those who come in Jesus' name is something Jesus instructed us to do. "I tell you the truth, whoever accepts anyone I send accepts me; and whoever accepts me accepts the one who sent me" (John 13:20). But the concept of the body reinforces the need to reverence the truth of the gospel living in every believer. That truth makes us one.

With Christ as the Head of the body, the rest is fitted together for a purpose God has in mind to impact the people around that body. Each man is strategically placed so that:

▸ He can use his God-given gifts to equip and serve the body to maximize its impact in the community;

▸ He can be shaped and equipped by the rest of the body who use their God-given gifts for that purpose.

Each member of the body must perform his or her function in order for the body to work according to God's purposes. Each member impacts the rest of the members. Our knowledge of how God works through the body must shape our attitudes and participation in the body. For instance, did you realize that the members of the body of Christ are members of Christ himself (1 Cor. 6:15)? Or that Jesus is the one who adds to our numbers

those who are being saved (Acts 2:47)? Did you know that it is
not only possible but absolutely desirable to have unity in the
body (Acts 4:32; Eph. 4:3)?

Equally important is the understanding that God gifts the
body for its common good, not so that every person can excel in
some way, but that the body is equipped for the purpose God is
directing, to reach a lost world with his love. Being recognized for
talents is not the same as being aware that God has equipped the
body with this gift to enable its obedience to him.

> ## How are you using the gifts God has given
> ## you to equip his saints for ministry?

Look at the body from God's perspective. "The body is a unit,
though it is made up of many parts. . . . God has combined the
members of the body . . . so that there should be no division in the
body, but that its parts should have equal concern for each other.
If one part suffers, every part suffers with it; if one part is honored,
every part rejoices with it. Now you are the body of Christ, and
each one of you is a part of it" (1 Cor. 12:12, 24–27).

As far as I can tell, Christ has no other way to redeem a lost and
spiritually decaying world than the Holy Spirit's working
through his body, the church. What are you currently doing in
his church? How are you using the gifts God has given you to
equip his saints for ministry?

"It was he who gave some to be apostles, some to be prophets,
some to be evangelists, and some to be pastors and teachers, to
prepare God's people for works of service, so that the body of
Christ may be built up until we all reach unity in the faith and in

the knowledge of the Son of God and become mature, attaining to the whole measure of the fullness of Christ. . . . We will in all things grow up into him who is the Head, that is, Christ. From him the whole body, joined and held together by every support-ing ligament, grows and builds itself up in love, as each part does its work" (Eph. 4:11—13, 15—16).

Do you see the importance of using your talents and gifts to build up the body of Christ, to prepare and equip its members for works of service, to promote unity and love between mem-bers in your church under Christ's leadership?

If you want to know what a church looks like that does not fol-low these guidelines, look at the story of Ananias and Sapphira (Acts 5:1—11) to see how God treats those in his church who are consumed by selfish desires. Look to the result of Achan's sin of covetousness (Josh. 7; 22:20) and how it affected the whole com-munity. The Israelite army was routed at Ai, and many people died because of Achan's secret disobedience to God's com-mands. Look to see what Christ has to say to his churches in Revelation 2—3. Many in the church had lost their first love and followed after their own immoral desires. When members of the body are dysfunctional in their roles, the entire body is compro-mised in its usefulness and effectiveness in God's kingdom. Each functions "according to the grace given" to him (Rom. 12:6). Do not receive the grace of God in vain! (2 Cor. 6:1).

The church works together under the leadership of Christ as the Head to accomplish mighty and amazing feats through his power and leadership. "'As you sent me into the world, I have sent them into the world'" (John 17:18).

A church that functions properly as a body of Christ will be characterized by several things.

▸ Members care for one another in love and carry each other's burdens.

▸ Members equip, encourage, undergird, and protect one another with the Holy Spirit's help.

▸ Members do together through the power of Christ what they could not possibly do alone.

▸ Members serve as Christ's hands, feet, and messengers, impacting communities, countries, and the world.

▸ Members become living bodies of Christ, demonstrating the nature and character of Christ for all to see.

▸ Members become obedient to the Father, and he will use them to carry out his mission to take the gospel to every person in every area of the world. Christ will live out his life obeying the Father, through his people, to continue his mission of redemption and reconciliation.

▸ Members continue to grow, mature, and reproduce themselves as a church in other places. The church has offspring by planting other churches.

A church in Georgia was determined to be a people on mission with God. Led by their pastor, staff, and church leaders, they began to obey God every time he spoke to them. They were obedient in evangelism, financial giving, and mission activities. God began working in members' hearts concerning international missions and specifically in the hearts of one of their finest couples. God led them to an unreached people group in West Africa, the Massai. The church commissioned the couple, and they were sent through their denomination's mission agency. The church began an incredible pilgrimage.

The church developed an extensive prayer ministry to support the couple and planned mission trips and mission giving to partner with them. At the same time, several other churches and missionary couples responded to the same calling. In a few years, the Massai began to respond. Today they have gone from almost no believers to more than 150,000 who have professed faith in Christ. Scores of Massai Christian churches have been established, and now the Massai are going to great lengths to take the gospel to others!

> THE MARK OF A CHRISTIAN IS
> TO LOVE HIS FELLOW BELIEVER.

But it didn't end there. This couple, with their children, have now gone to another large unreached people group, the Karamajing. God is using them to bring thousands to himself. The couple's home church continues to pray, give, and go to other areas of the world as workers together with God. They have not stopped being on mission with God, just as God intended. God intends for your church and you to be on mission with him. He is not through using his people to reach a world. We are God's strategy.

A church in an African country had a prison warden in their congregation. Members prayed for him and encouraged him. Through the constant support and encouragement of his church, the warden began prayer groups, Bible studies, and evangelistic crusades at his prison. Many prisoners have come to Christ because this ordinary man was faithful to his Lord and because his church took seriously their role as the body of

Christ, supporting each member in their God-given call. With this oneness the apostles also shared with all who would listen. "In the temple courts and from house to house, they never stopped teaching and proclaiming the good news that Jesus is the Christ" (Acts 5:42).

This is God's pattern for every generation! The greatest moments in history for God's people have come when his people have sought him in prayer and obeyed him with boldness. "After they prayed, the place where they were meeting was shaken. And they were all filled with the Holy Spirit and spoke the word of God boldly. All the believers were one in heart and mind" (Acts 4:31–32). The result has been people becoming missionaries, going wherever they needed to go. God desires to use his people everywhere and in every situation.

THE MARK OF A DISCIPLE

People knew Peter was Jesus' disciple primarily because he was continually with Jesus, following him and participating with him. Today a disciple of Jesus follows Christ and continually participates in his activity wherever it leads.

Shortly after Glenn became manager of a manufacturing facility in Nevada, he learned that Bob, an employee, had been in a serious drug-related car accident. After a time away for recovery, Bob returned to work showing some improvement after having "learned his lesson." But eventually, drug-related problems began to occur at work, and other employees refused to work with Bob, saying he was unsafe and shouldn't be on the job.

After several unheeded warnings, Bob was fired. He immediately filed a grievance with the union. The meeting between the union official, Bob, and Glenn went on at length and seemed to go nowhere. Finally, Glenn said, "Bob, you have a problem. You know you have a problem. You need help, and I know just the one who can give this help to you."

> WE OWE A GREAT DEAL TO THE FAITHFUL PRAYERS
> OF MANY DURING OUR TIMES OF NEED.

The union official asked to be excused, and Glenn shared with Bob about Jesus Christ and how Bob could come to know him personally. Glenn gave Bob something to read on how to have peace with God and asked him to go through it at home. The next day Bob dropped the grievance. A change had begun in his heart. It is possible for an ordinary plant manager, even in the hostile environment of a grievance meeting, to share the gospel with someone who needs the Lord.

LISTEN FOR GOD'S VOICE

Christ says he knows us, will call us by name, and we will recognize and respond to his voice. Our role is to be listening for him when he speaks. What a tragedy it would be for us to miss a crucial word from the Master at a critical time in our lives because we were distracted by worldly matters. Will Christ pass us by and go on to one who is listening? Will we miss the tremendous blessing God is holding for us because we are inattentive to him at a decisive moment?

How can we be sure that we recognize God's voice when he speaks to us? Perhaps more importantly, how can you be sure that you are listening when God speaks to you?

John 10:3–6, 14 contains principles that come down to being familiar enough with God and his Word to recognize and obey him when he speaks. "The watchman opens the gate for him, and the sheep listen to his voice. He calls his own sheep by name and leads them out. When he has brought out all his own, he goes on ahead of them, and his sheep follow him because they know his voice. But they will never follow a stranger; in fact, they will run away from him because they do not recognize a stranger's voice." Jesus used this figure of speech, but they did not understand what he was telling them. "I am the good shepherd; I know my sheep and my sheep know me" (John 10:3–5, 14).

It sounds simple, but it is simple only if we are prepared to hear God and become familiar with his voice. Several times Jesus said, "He who has ears, let him hear" (Matt. 11:15). Jesus meant there was more than one application to the story. There was an obvious meaning, and there was a spiritual application. Jesus emphasized that there was a chance his hearers might not catch what he was trying to tell them.

Jesus often spoke in parables so that those with spiritual insights would grasp the spiritual application, but those who had no spiritual inclination would only grasp the obvious meanings. If our hearts are right with God, we will grasp what the Scripture is telling us, and we will hear the Shepherd's voice. If our hearts are not in tune with God, we will miss the Shepherd's message.

LOVE ONE ANOTHER

It is easy to love people we are already close to. If we love with God's love, we have to include all those unknown to us or in need of help. This broadens our responsibility when we think of who constitutes "others" when it comes to expressing love. Strangers and prisoners are to be loved as if we were in their situation. "Keep on loving each other as brothers. Do not forget to entertain strangers, for by so doing some people have entertained angels without knowing it. Remember those in prison as if you were their fellow prisoners, and those who are mistreated as if you yourselves were suffering" (Heb. 13:1–3).

> IF OUR HEARTS ARE RIGHT WITH GOD, WE WILL
> GRASP WHAT THE SCRIPTURE IS TELLING US, AND
> WE WILL HEAR THE SHEPHERD'S VOICE.

The apostle Paul always worked in relation to the churches. Paul was not an independent agent of God doing his own thing. He was integrally attached to the support, prayer, and encouragement of the churches. Peter was sent from a local body of believers to check out the Gentile worship and report back to verify the activity of the Holy Spirit there. The principle here is that wherever an individual member of the body of Christ goes, he goes as part of the body. And, if he is part of the body, he is also connected to the Head of the body, which is Christ. So the response of others to a member of the body is also their response to Christ. "'I tell you the truth, whoever accepts anyone I send accepts me; and whoever accepts me accepts the one who sent me'" (John 13:20).

The body of Christ never cancels out the individual; rather, the individual finds his true purpose and meaning expressed through the group. Imagine an eye trying to function without the rest of the body. Absurd! How about a hand or a foot apart from the arm or leg? Impossible. Just as impossible is a Christian apart from a local church!

You are an individual, but you function within a body of believers. Your role is critically important to the life of the body. The body sees the members as an integral part of the body. The body undergirds the members in the ministry God has called them to, helps clarify what God is saying to them in relation to the body, and allows them to help equip one another for service with God.

THE MAN GOD USES IN HIS LARGER KINGDOM

When God takes an ordinary man who is yielded to him, that person acts as leaven to affect his community, city, and world. Just as yeast spreads through all of the dough, God's people can make a difference.

God's people are the best people in the world! I've traveled the world and visited God's best servants in some of the most remote places of his kingdom. I am always amazed, inspired, and humbled at the loyalty and commitment of God's people who serve in difficult and dangerous places. But the most amazing part is that I can become an instant brother and develop a close bond with any of these men and women regardless of their nationality, responsibilities, language, or age because we all serve the same Lord.

When you allow Christ to be your Savior and Lord, you not only become a part of a body of believers where you live, you gain membership to a worldwide network of God's people. This was never more meaningful to me personally than when our family needed prayers for my daughter who had been diagnosed with cancer. We were deeply encouraged by the many letters, calls, and notes from those who were praying for us around the world. People we had never met were interceding on our behalf before our heavenly Father. We owe a great deal to the faithful prayers of many during our times of need.

> ONE ACT OF OBEDIENCE CAN BE THE SIGNAL TO
> THOUSANDS OF OTHERS WHO HAVE BEEN SENSING
> GOD IS UP TO SOMETHING IN THEIR LIVES.

God has his people placed strategically all around the world, serving him in important ways. Some of the ways may appear insignificant on the outside, but they may be the key to God's plans. One man drilling a well in West Africa may not appear to have much significance. But when you understand that God had called him and commissioned him, you realize that much more is at stake. It's not what we do that is important but what God can accomplish through what we do.

Ezekiel 22:30 does not say that God is looking for someone with vast influence, intelligence, family connections, or position. It says God is looking for one man among others who will serve his purpose, realizing the value of what God has created, and interceding for others so they might not face the consequences of their actions. "'I looked for a man among them who would build up the wall and stand before me in the gap on behalf of the land so I would not have to destroy it, but I found none'" (Ezek. 22:30).

Are you such a man? Could your earnest desire to make Christ real to someone be the service that opens a household to the gospel or triggers a ministry that will bless many? It could happen, not because of your potential but because of God's ability.

One Christian man sent out a plea for used eyeglasses to distribute in underdeveloped countries. His aim was to help people see physically and spiritually. His obedience to God inspired other Christian optometrists who helped collect more than four thousand pairs of glasses for distribution in South American countries. Remember that the individual is connected to the larger kingdom of God. God can martial his forces in any country at any time if they are ready and willing to listen and obey. One act of obedience can be the signal to thousands of others who have been sensing God is up to something in their lives.

I remember meeting Olen Miles, a retired building contractor. That humble, hard-working man gave a major part of his life volunteering to build churches. Not only did his own state benefit from his years of service, but several other countries also have the permanent mark of Olen Miles on their landscapes. Thousands of people worship today and attend theological classes in buildings built because of his faithfulness and obedience to God. His life inspired many other men to volunteer in building churches and seminary buildings as well.

It only takes one man obedient to the God-given vision of ministry to inspire others. And more people have been introduced to Christ by the faithfulness of ordinary people than all the famous evangelists combined! God uses ordinary people in extraordinary ways, because he is a part of it.

Being on mission with God is a worldwide effort. An engineer in Montana can assist Christian brothers in Russia; a Christian doctor from Saskatchewan can spend two and a half years in a Yemen hospital; or a pastor from Argentina can help a small mission church in Vancouver reach the Spanish-speaking people who live there. Thousands of scenarios are lived out every day because of how God's economy works. We are individuals and a part of the living body of Christ. We work together with other believers in his larger kingdom to accomplish God's purposes.

> BEING ON MISSION WITH GOD
> IS A WORLDWIDE EFFORT.

Churches who are proud of their independence or self-reliance never experience the joy of accessing God's kingdom resources to impact a world. They only see their impact reaching to the end of their membership, their resources, and no further. For Christians to be obedient to Christ's command to "'go into all the world and preach the good news to all creation'" (Mark 16:15) takes a cooperative effort across church and denominational lines and channels of blessing throughout the larger kingdom of God. The Canadian churches I was a part of for most of my pastoral ministry were deeply affected by church youth choirs, college drama teams, senior adult volunteer workers, and many others that came from the United States every year. Several churches that stand today across Canada were built by the funds and the sweat of American brothers and sisters who accepted God's invitation to be part of what he was doing on the other side of the border.

THE CHRISTIAN COMMUNITY

God uses men around the world, but he also uses men to affect the Christian community close by. This is also part of God's larger kingdom.

The mark of a Christian is to love his fellow believer. It is not how many souls are saved or how much you sacrifice. Jesus says the world will be able to tell you are a follower of Christ by your love for your Christian brother. If you have any relationship with a fellow believer that is not consistent with the type of love Christ demonstrated for you, set it right immediately. If you cannot demonstrate love for one in whom Christ lives, you can't properly love anyone who is apart from him. "'A new command I give you: Love one another.... By this all men will know that you are my disciples, if you love one another'" (John 13:34–35).

I visited a fellow pastor of another denomination one day. When he opened the door, I could tell he'd been weeping. He shared that the night before he had been in a difficult meeting with his deacons only to come home to find his teenage son had left home. I ministered to the pastor, brought my deacons to minister to his deacons, my wife to minister to his wife, and our teenagers to minister to his teenagers. His ministry had been in the balance, but through encouragement, love, and prayer, a church was salvaged and came to know practically what John 13:34–35 means. Remember Christ's words, "'Whatever you did for one of the least of these brothers of mine, you did for me'"

(Matt. 25:40). It is Christ we are serving, and it is Christ we are ministering to when we love our fellow believers.

FAMILY LIFE

God also uses men in his larger kingdom as he guides men in their families.

My sons once said to me, "Dad, we don't think you realize how many times we could have gone off track, but we just couldn't bring ourselves to hurt you and mom that way."

I replied, "Well, the reverse is true too. There were many times your dad could have done the wrong things, but I just couldn't hurt you boys." I have withheld from doing things and moving in certain directions in my life because I knew it would influence my children. Scripture says that the sins of the father will be passed on to the children and the grandchildren. I am totally convinced this is true. The chance my children and grandchildren have may well rest on my walk with God. That has been a restraining influence on my life.

> MEN OUGHT TO BE PRAYING FOR
> ONE ANOTHER, PERIOD!

Few men are taught how to be good fathers or husbands. There either is not enough time, or men are not aware of studies on parenting and relationship development. A man who is wise will seek out others who can hold him accountable and hold him to his commitments in his marriage and home life. Men ought to be praying for one another's families, marriages, and job situations. Men ought to be praying for one another, period!

If you take seriously the implementing of "'seek first his kingdom and his righteousness'" (Matt. 6:33), your life will be noticeably different. You will stand out among peers as one who knows God and trusts him with your life and the lives of your family. The first people who ought to see us as authentic Christians are our children. Your life will be transformed daily by the living Lord, and there will be a radical difference.

SUMMARY

Many great movements of God—biblically and historically—manifested the activity of God in and through men! God chooses, calls, and sends men. God uses them individually, corporately, in concert together with their circumstances and obedience. God looks for men with hearts completely yielded to him. God is profoundly active. Our lives are the product of choices we have made in our encounters with God. In those choices God can take the ordinary and, through his presence in and through them, make us and our opportunities extraordinary.

My son Tom and I shall continue to pray for God's mighty anointing on you and all the men who read and study this book. Join us in praying for the men around you as we become men God can use.

THINK ABOUT—PRAY ABOUT

God intends for us to acknowledge the presence of Jesus Christ in every area of our lives. This is the most fundamental of principles for Christians. Whatever we may be doing or wherever we may be, we must realize and acknowledge Jesus Christ's presence and activity working in us, through us, and around us. We must see every situation in which we find ourselves as a means of obtaining a greater knowledge of Jesus Christ.

▸ Pray to become the man God can use. Pray specifically for a greater understanding of what it means to be God's people.

▸ Men who do not truly worship cannot truly serve God. Pray that you will grow in your worship. Worship is at the heart of your relationship with God. Out of worship God will reveal himself and his will. More happens out of an encounter with God through times of worship than any other time in our lives.

▸ Missionaries come from our churches. They enter every walk of life on assignment for God. Take inventory of men in your church—young men, teens, boys—to see God's present and potential missionaries! Pray for them and commit to encourage and support them in their missionary assignments.

▸ The Great Commission was given to the body of Christ and to each member: "'Therefore go and make disciples of all nations, baptizing them in the name of the Father and of the Son and of the Holy Spirit, and teaching them to obey everything I have commanded you. And surely I am with you always, to the very end of the age'" (Matt. 28:19–20). Pray and thank God that you function with the body on mission according to the grace he has given and you have received, as a man God uses.

---

1. Dr. J. Edwin Orr, transcribed from 24 January 1974 lecture, Southwestern Baptist Theological Seminary, Ft. Worth, Texas, chapel service.

2. Ibid.

3. *Share Jesus Without Fear Kit* (Nashville: LifeWay Press, 1997), videotape session 4.

GROUP DISCUSSION GUIDE: CONDUCTING A GROUP STUDY OF *THE MAN GOD USES*

The Group Study Guide on the following pages includes:
- Good ideas for group members
- Easy-to-use group session plans

Read both before you plan for your men's group.

GROUP MEMBER IDEAS

Who? A small group study of *The Man God Uses* is appropriate for men's home groups, Bible study groups, accountability groups, discipleship and prayer groups, and one-to-one discipling. The topic and time will benefit men of all ages.

When? Get together at a time that works for your group. The sessions plans aim for about an hour of discussion and prayer. However, allow the Holy Spirit to determine your schedule. The plans in this section serve as a framework; your goal should be to meet the needs of the men in your group.

Where? Men can meet at the church, in a home or business, for a meal at a local restaurant, or anywhere conducive for discussion and prayer.

How? Use the group plans in this section. Before each group session, as a group member you should:

▸ Pray for each group member.
▸ Study the chapter the group will discuss.
▸ Encourage men in the group.
▸ Get in touch right away with men who miss a session.

God bless you as you facilitate your men's group.

CHAPTER 1
THE CHARACTER OF THE MAN GOD USES

1. Begin on time. Make latecomers welcome with as little interruption as possible. Provide name tags during the first group session unless your men know one another well.
2. Ask each man to introduce himself and briefly tell one way God has blessed him during the past week.
3. Say: "Recognizing God's blessing is one way of responding to God. Calling on him to meet our needs is another kind of response." Invite men to pray silently, thanking and asking God for whatever is on their hearts. After a time of silent prayer, ask God to guide the session.
4. Say: "In Chapter 1, it says, 'Each man God used had a responsive heart ready to hear God and a life that was available to obey God. They also possessed the integrity to

honor God.' What comes to mind when you apply the concepts 'available to obey God' and 'integrity to honor God' to your life?" Describe moments of success, struggle, or confusion in dealing with these ideas.

5. Lead the group to brainstorm ways men can be more available to obey God. Write your group's list on a poster or large sheet of paper. Add to the list throughout the session.

6. Ask, "What are the similarities and differences men see in the kind of integrity that honors God and the standard for integrity in their workplaces?"

7. Ask: "Does culture give us a false definition of what a man's character should be? How does culture's definition of success differ from the way God defines success?"

8. Invite the men to list the signs of a spiritually healthy man based on Psalm 15. Instruct men to pair up and share one area of spiritual health and one area that needs their attention. Allow several minutes for sharing.

9. Reconvene the group and say: "Telling the truth, keeping promises, and not cheating or hurting others are all values in our culture. Why do you think these traits of a spiritually healthy man are not more common among men in our culture?"

10. Ask the following questions, allowing time for response to each question:

   ▸ Can a man change his heart?
   ▸ What would it take for a man to try to make the kind of heart change that only God can make?
   ▸ Why would anyone trust his own power instead of God's?

11. Say: "Hebrews 4:12–13 says that God's Word judges our thoughts and attitudes. Why does that idea make most people uncomfortable?"

12. Say, "One of the wonderful things about God is his power to transform us." Invite someone to read Ephesians 4:22–24 to the group. Ask the group to interpret what this verse teaches about who we are in Christ.

13. Encourage the men to commit to pray for one another's integrity of heart throughout the coming weeks. Ask men to seal their commitments by expressing them in a time of sentence prayer.

CHAPTER 2
HOW GOD SHAPES A MAN

1. As the group gathers, ask each man to reflect on how God has shaped him through the past week. Honor each man's time commitment by starting on time. Invite several men to report briefly on the shaping activity of God in their lives.

2. Say, "Chapter 2 dealt with tough circumstances in life." Ask for prayer needs or praises related to things that are making life difficult. Ask men to pray in pairs for the circumstances that have been mentioned, as well as for others they may be aware of.

3. Say: "God can use each life experience to deepen our dependence on him. In times of crisis, we cry out to God for strength, wisdom, help, or answers in the midst of our situation. We recognize that God alone is truly able to handle what we face, and that we depend on his love for us, his pro-

tection, and his guidance. God can use each day both to teach and to deliver us from whatever the day may bring."

4. Ask the group to recount times when they have experienced God's protection or guidance. Allow several men to share. Then say: "The ability to trust God in every circumstance is a result of a Spirit-filled life. The Holy Spirit is present in every believer. Because of the Spirit's presence, we have access to wisdom and comfort."

5. Ask, "Does our lack of patience or quickness to declare success or failure limit our availability to God's shaping?"

6. Tell what a Christian is and how a person becomes a Christian. It may be that some men in your group think they are Christians simply because they attend church or read the Bible or give money to the church. Give several men a chance to share their spiritual journeys and how they came to the point in their lives that they:

> Recognized they were sinners separated from God because of sin. "For all have sinned and fall short of the glory of God" (Rom. 3:23).

> Confessed their sins to God and asked his forgiveness. "If we confess our sins, he is faithful and just and will forgive us our sins and purify us from all unrighteousness" (1 John 1:9).

> Acknowledged Jesus Christ's right to be Lord of their lives, and freely gave him control of their lives forevermore, and in return accepted his free gift of salvation. "If you confess with your mouth, 'Jesus is Lord,' and believe in your heart that God raised him from the dead, you will be saved. For it is with your heart that

you believe and are justified, and it is with your mouth that you confess and are saved" (Rom. 10:9–10).

7.   Share the following illustration as a final thought. "He was a man who feared God and turned away from evil. No wonder Satan had it in for him! Job determined to remain unapproachable to evil. Even when everything he had was eventually taken from him, including his own health, his character held out. He remained faithful to the end, even when he didn't have a clue what God was up to. God blessed him because of his integrity."

8.   Read aloud Jeremiah 29:11. Invite men to tell what this verse says about their relationships to God. "'I know the plans I have for you' declares the Lord, 'plans to prosper you and not to harm you, plans to give you hope and a future'" (Jer. 29:11).

9.   Ask men to pair up for a closing time of prayer. Invite each man to begin his prayer by stating or paraphrasing Isaiah 64:8:

> O LORD, you are our Father.
> We are the clay, you are the potter;
> we are all the work of your hand.

CHAPTER 3
GOD'S REFINING PROCESS

1.   As the men arrive, give them an encouraging greeting that compliments qualities or characteristics they possess.

2.   Begin on time. Say: "Do you realize that God could use any of us or all of us to do anything he purposed to do? Even

though I affirmed each one of you as you arrived, that affirmation was only based on what you could humanly perceive. The Creator, by contrast, continuously does what we could never imagine."

3. Say: "Those who will, pray sentence prayers for God to convict us of our sins and lead us to repentance. Sin renders us useless to God. As we pray, remember the sins of pride, arrogance, greed, laziness, and disobedience to God."

4. Read 1 Samuel 15:22–23.

> "Does the LORD delight in burnt offerings and sacrifices
>   as much as in obeying the voice of the LORD?
> To obey is better than sacrifice,
>   and to heed is better than the fat of rams.
> For rebellion is like the sin of divination,
>   and arrogance like the evil of idolatry.
> Because you have rejected the word of the LORD,
>   he has rejected you as king."

Say: "King Saul's pride led to the beginning of his downfall. In this passage he has lied to Samuel and to God. Do you agree or disagree that it is better to obey than sacrifice? How can one sin often lead to other more devastating sins?" Bring into the discussion how sin can cause God to move on to someone else with opportunities to serve him. Allow time for discussion.

5. Ask: "What is your reaction to the fact that God spent years preparing Joseph through hardships to be a ruler of the Egyptians and the avenue of survival for his family?

How long might any of us have to wait to see God's will manifested?"

6. Review chapter 3's key points by reminding the group that Christ first chose us, appointed us, and instructed us to bear fruit. Invite men to testify to the impact on their lives of being chosen by Christ. Ask them to talk about their sense of appointment and how that relates to the "appointment" of missionaries, pastors, deacons, and teachers. Ask the men to tell about people they know whose lives bear fruit for God.

7. Read Matthew 12:25 and Matthew 18:19–20 to the group. "'Every kingdom divided against itself will be ruined, and every city or household divided against itself will not stand'" (Matt. 12:25). "'Again, I tell you that if two of you on earth agree about anything you ask for, it will be done for you by my Father in heaven. For where two or three come together in my name, there am I with them'" (Matt. 18:19–20).

Say: "Contrast these verses. Then make comparisons between these verses and (1) churches that function like a household divided, and (2) churches that come together in Christ's name and are honored with his presence."

8. Say: "The issue of unity is of extreme importance to God and in the life and usefulness of his church. We would have to fight against the prayers and the glory of Jesus Christ himself to bring deliberate strife or disunity into our relationships with others. How can we bring about unity?"

9. Ask men to stand in a circle with arms around one another's shoulders or waists. Call on three men to pray. Ask one

man to pray to remove anything that divides us from God's purpose. Ask another man to thank God for the unity his Spirit brings. Ask the third man to pray as they go out as men appointed to bear spiritual fruit.

CHAPTER 4
THE GODLY MAN'S RESPONSE TO GOD

1. As each man arrives, ask: "Whom did God use most in bringing you to salvation? Who shared the gospel message with you?"

2. Begin on time. Ask several men to share their answers to the questions you asked as they arrived. Keep the sharing moving, and don't allow one man to dominate the time.

3. Say, "Those who will, pray sentence prayers, thanking God specifically for those people who shared the gospel with you."

4. Ask: "Do you take personal responsibility for your relationship with God, or do you depend on others, such as your pastor, wife, Bible study leader, or Sunday school teacher, to cause you to grow? What does it mean to take personal responsibility for your own spiritual growth?"

5. Say: "The man God uses is always first encountered by God. If God chooses to make his presence known, it is incredibly important that you recognize that it's God and recognize what he's saying to you. What kinds of things have you heard of God saying to men, either in the Bible, or in your experiences?"

6. Assign each man in the group one or more of the following Scriptures. Say, "Listen as each passage is read to see the

different facets and benefits that fearing God brings." Read
the verses one after another with no comment.

Psalm 15:4	Psalm 111:5, 10
Psalm 25:14	Psalm 112:1
Psalm 31:19	Psalm 119:74
Psalm 33:18	Psalm 145:19
Psalm 34:7	Psalm 147:11
Psalm 85:9	Proverbs 8:13
Psalm 103:11	Proverbs 10:27

7. Say, "Fear is only one way a godly man responds to God.
   What other ways does a godly man respond to God?"
   (Submits to God; totally obeys in faith; is accountable; has
   joy; humility; is an encouragement to others.) Briefly discuss these and other responses men identify.

8. Say: "Your relationship with God affects all your other relationships. In what ways is your obedience to Christ affect-
   ing your marriage? your children? your workplace? your
   community?" Allow sufficient time to discuss each area.

9. Form groups of three and invite each man in each group to
   pray for one another's obedience in all areas of life.

CHAPTER 5
MADE FOR TIMES OF CRISIS

1. Before the group session, enlist one or two men to be prepared to thank God for demonstrating his power during a
   crisis time that happened in the church or in his personal
   life.

2. As the group arrives, distribute items that are useful in an emergency such as flashlight batteries; coins for pay phones; aspirin; emergency phone numbers for police, fire, ambulance, poison-control, etc.

3. Begin on time. Say: "It is natural to experience crises in our lives. In fact, some ordinary events turn into crises when we realize we don't have something we need such as fresh batteries or a phone number. The more ready we can be when a crisis comes, the more likely we are able to respond and limit the negative effects. The man God uses is made for times of crisis because God has prepared him in advance."

4. Call on the men you enlisted in advance to thank God for demonstrating his power during a crisis time that was experienced by the church family or in their personal lives.

5. Read John 17:3: "Now this is eternal life: that they may know you, the only true God, and Jesus Christ, whom you have sent."

   Ask the men to discuss the passage. Say, "If only eternal things last, and God's Word tells us that the key to eternal life is knowing God through his Son Jesus, whom he sent to us, how could we apply that standard of importance to everything we do?" Consider the implications for family, work, worship, prayer, and your church's priorities.

6. Ask, "What effect does it have on believers to discover that God wants to prepare them so he can work through them in times of crisis?"

Ask, "What is the eternal significance of the way we allow God to work through us in times of crisis?" Consider the impact of our obedience on the spiritual legacy we leave our families, congregation, and community.

7. Review chapter 5's key points by reminding the group that a crisis of belief equals a moment of decision; a crisis is an opportunity; and a church is a family created to act in times of crisis. Ask, "How does a crisis of belief represent a moment of decision about whether we will trust and obey God in a particular situation?"

8. Share this list about how God used men in times of crisis and the result of their obedience to God.

MEN	RESULTS
Noah (Gen. 6–9)	Preserved God's people
Abraham (Gen. 12)	Began God's people
Moses (Exod. 2–12)	Delivered God's people
David (1 Sam. 16–24)	Gave God's people a king
Jeremiah (Jer. 1:5)	Warned God's people
The Disciples (Acts 2:42–47)	Began God's church
Paul (Rom. 11:13)	Reached the Gentiles

9. Divide the men into three smaller groups. Instruct each group to select one of the Scripture examples from the matching exercise. Make sure no two groups select the same example. Instruct the subgroups to explore and summarize for the entire group how God used the example they selected in times of crisis and the result of being

obedient to God. Say, "Hearing about and retelling God's mighty acts both affirm and equip us for times of crisis."

10. Read John 14:2—3: "'In my Father's house are many rooms; if it were not so, I would have told you. I am going there to prepare a place for you. And if I go and prepare a place for you, I will come back and take you to be with me that you also may be where I am.'"

    Ask, "In what way does the certainty of Christ's return create a crisis to which we must respond?"

11. Ask group members to gather in pairs to pray for one another. Before praying, invite them to share with their prayer partner any crisis they are facing. Encourage each man to respond with Scripture used in chapter 5 as a way to encourage and affirm one another.

CHAPTER 6
BEING A KINGDOM CITIZEN

1. Begin on time. Read Isaiah 55:8—9:

    "'For my thoughts are not your thoughts,
    neither are your ways my ways,"
    declares the LORD.

    'As the heavens are higher than the earth,
            so are my ways higher than your ways
        and my thoughts than your thoughts.'"

    Ask, "How can we know God's thoughts and ways?"

2. Invite the men to bow their heads while you read Hebrews 11:32–38 from your Bible. Ask them to meditate on this passage and silently pray that they will live obediently to whatever God requires of them.

3. Say: "We know that God's ways differ from the world's ways. Man is always aware of time and his desires. God is not bound by time, and his greatest desire is to draw all people to himself. When God involves us in his purposes, he may reveal himself to others by our witness, both through the abundance that comes from him and by the sufferings he strengthens us to bear. In every situation, our response to God is a witness to the world that God loves them. By our love and trust, regardless of circumstance, we show that God is worthy of their love and trust."

   Remind the men of the Hebrews passage you read during the prayer time. Ask them to discuss examples of witnesses that have shaped their lives or have resulted in others' coming to God through Christ.

4. Say: "The world we live in tells us to have pride, but the Bible tells us to be humble. The world says to be professional, while the Bible says to be a servant. The world says not to proceed unless you are certain of the means, but God says that if we are obeying him we can trust him to supply our needs. How can we function as kingdom citizens in today's world?"

5. Say: "Like disobedience, obedience also has a price. As people who belong to the kingdom, we can better understand why Jesus, our Savior and example, would allow himself to be taken, tortured, and crucified to pay for our sins." Discuss the price of obedience.

6. Review the key concepts from chapter 6. As you read the following statements, invite members to share insights or questions they have.

    ▸ The world's ways are not God's ways.
    ▸ Being a kingdom citizen means functioning according to kingdom ways.
    ▸ Truth is only fully understood through the person of Jesus Christ.
    ▸ Faith accesses the power of God in any situation.
    ▸ Wherever God's people are, all that is available from God is also present, including his wisdom, power, grace, and patience.

7. Read John 14:6 to the group: "'I am the way and the truth and the life. No one comes to the Father except through me.'"

    Ask them to repeat the verse in unison. Say: "This verse from God's Word tells us that Jesus is the way, the truth, and the life. It also tells us that the way we come to the Father is through Jesus. The next verse, John 14:7, tells us that if we really know Jesus, we know God the Father as well."

8. Read John 14:7: "'If you really knew me, you would know my Father as well. From now on, you do know him and have seen him.'"

    Ask, "From knowing Jesus, what do you know now about God?" Create a list, or have someone write down the men's responses. When the discussion ends, read the list as a summary of the group's experience with God.

9. Ask the group to bow their heads and listen as you read Isaiah 53:11−12 from your Bible. Ask the group to reflect on God's perspective as he provided forgiveness for our sins through the obedience of his Son. After several moments of silence, pray aloud that God would make these verses a part of each man's life and that each man would live this truth.

CHAPTER 7
ON MISSION WITH GOD IN OUR WORLD

1. Give each man a piece of paper and a pencil as he arrives and ask him to list five places he has been or activities he has been involved in during the last twenty-four hours.
2. Begin on time. Ask the men to list other places or activities if they want so that nothing is left out. The group will be praying over these lists. Collect the lists.
3. Place the lists in the center of the group. Say, "These lists represent opportunities, mission points, and places where God could and does desire to use you." Begin the prayer by praying aloud for opportunities and the group's willingness to respond. Close with a time of silent prayer.
4. Say: "Faithfulness can seem incredibly difficult. Part of the reason is that we are to stay faithful to God at all times. The hardest part is probably not resisting temptation, unless it is the temptation to be impatient. 'Long obedience' seems especially hard in a sped-up, modern world. Yet years seemed long in ancient times as well."
5. Read Joshua 14:9−10 from your Bible. Say: "When we don't see results as quickly as we expect, it does not mean

the mission is over or has failed. It means that God is not bound by time, yet his timing is perfect, and in time, he will accomplish his purpose."

6. Say: "God is on mission, and he has invited us to join him. How are you currently on mission in your family, in your workplace, or in your other relationships? How could you join God more actively on his mission?"

7. Say: "The Bible tells us to seek God's kingdom first in all we do (Matt. 6:33). The time to do that is not limited to the beginning of a mission, as we try to understand and comply with God's plans, but also as difficulties arise." Ask the group how they could go about seeking God's kingdom when they encounter the following:

    ‣ When other believers drop out of being on mission
    ‣ When we realize we have been distracted or compromised
    ‣ When enemies arise
    ‣ When doubts and fears arise
    ‣ When circumstance increases difficulty
    ‣ When we become overworked and tired
    ‣ When a compromise is offered
    ‣ When we have failed at our attempts
    ‣ When we are not recognized or appreciated

8. Say: "All God's resources are available to us as we serve his purpose. Not the least of these are the believers he has surrounded us with in our churches and the gifts he has provided for the church through them." Ask one of the men to read Colossians 1:18, 21–22 to the group. Ask: "What did it cost Christ to create his church? Who is the head of

the church? If our duty and service is focused on following the head (Christ), can we fail as long as we continue, regardless of the circumstances we encounter?"

9. Summarize the discussion by reading Ephesians 5:25–27 from your Bible as a description of how much Christ loves us and wants us to join together to serve him. Ask, "If people usually live up to expectations, how could our congregation's taking Christ's view of us as holy and blameless affect actions and activities as we work and worship together?"

10. Ask the men to name people God used to make himself real in their lives and influence their relationship with God. Ask the men to consider the legacy they are leaving those who come after them.

11. Make the closing prayer time a time of commissioning. If the group is six men or fewer, ask one man to kneel and the group to lay hands on him as another group member voices a prayer of commissioning for him. Repeat the process with each man. If the group is larger, join hands or place arms around shoulders in a circle as sentence prayers of commissioning are offered on behalf of the group by the men in the group. A group member should close the time by thanking God for each of the men present and by asking a special portion of yieldedness to God for each man.